A GUIDE TO
STUDENT
SUCCESS
IN COLLEGE

WILLIAM R. HARVEY

Kendall Hunt
publishing company

Kendall Hunt
publishing company

www.kendallhunt.com
Send all inquiries to:
4050 Westmark Drive
Dubuque, IA 52004-1840

Published in the United States of America

This book is dedicated to our children, Kelly Rene,
William Christopher, and Leslie Denise, who all have
undergraduate and graduate degrees from top-rated institutions of
higher education. More than that, my wife, Norma,
and I are exceedingly pleased that they are terrific professionals
who are leading first-class and outstanding personal lives.
They make us proud every day!

CONTENTS

FOREWORD

During my years of service at the United States Department of Education, Dr. Harvey, as the Chair of the President's Board of Advisors on HBCUs and President of Hampton University, significantly impacted key policy, regulatory, and operational matters that affected many colleges and universities—especially schools focused on social mobility. Bill constantly worked with and pushed the Administration, Secretary of Education, and other federal agencies to better support striving first generation, low-income, and under-resourced students. As an example, the Department of Education substantially modified its regulatory approach and operations so that tens of thousands of students and families were eligible for hundreds of millions of dollars in financial resources that would have otherwise been unavailable. Quietly but forcefully, Dr. Harvey has spent a lifetime of service, building a more inclusive and equitable post-secondary environment for the country. This has resulted in favorable outcomes for generations of striving students and families. It has been a pleasure working with Dr. Harvey and I continue to be impressed by his unwavering commitment to serve others.

James W. Runcie
United States Department of Education
Federal Student Aid—Chief Operating Officer (2010–17)

This is an absolutely excellent book by Dr. William R. Harvey which covers all aspects of Student Development Services for the past, present, and future. The book is so comprehensive that a copy should be in every library, as well as each person's home. Parents, faculty members, middle school, high school, college or university students, and institutional recruiters should definitely possess a copy of this outstanding book.

Dr. Harvey is a competent, experienced educator and administrator. As a great leader of Hampton University, he has improved every aspect of the University, which included, but has not been limited to, increasing the endowment, initiating numerous academic and research programs, constructing new facilities, increasing student enrollment and improving extracurricular programs. With the assistance of a very strong Board of Trustees, faculty, staff, and alumni organizations, and Dr. Harvey's visionary leadership at Hampton University, four satellites are orbiting the earth and Hampton has 100 percent control of a NASA mission. The University has also developed one of the few Proton Therapy Centers to treat cancer in the United States.

In spite of his very busy schedule, Dr. Harvey has always shared his experience and leadership qualities with other organizations and institutions. He has provided advice to numerous university presidents, and also presidents of the United States of America. He also chaired President Barack Obama's Advisory Board on the White House Initiative for Historically Black Colleges and Universities (HBCUs). During my sixteen-year tenure as an Executive with the Commission on Colleges of the Southern Association of Colleges and Schools, Dr. Harvey chaired more than thirty Reaffirmation Committees for Accreditation. We can all benefit from Dr. Harvey's extraordinary leadership and contributions to society.

Everyone needs a copy of this great book.

Joffre T. Whisenton, PhD
Former Southern University System of Louisiana President
Southern Association of Colleges
and Schools Accreditation Executive
GS 17 Special Assistant to the Secretary
of the U.S. Department of Health, Education and Welfare
Currently President of Joffre T. Whisenton
and Associates, Incorporated

CHAPTER I

INTRODUCTION

My work with young people has been long and varied as a high school history, civics, and government teacher; deputy director of an Office of Economic Opportunity Agency; Assistant to the Dean of the Graduate School of Education at Harvard University; Assistant to the President at Fisk University; Vice President for Student Affairs and Vice President for Administrative Services at Tuskegee University; and for over forty years, as President of Hampton University. Given my career-long experience with college-age students, I was asked to write on what it takes for a student to succeed in a higher educational enterprise.

Although I studied and was an assistant to the dean of the Harvard Graduate School of Education, my last three places of employment were Historically Black Colleges and Universities (HBCUs) (Fisk, Tuskegee, and Hampton). Therefore, much of my thinking was developed as a result of the values, standards, and role-modeling I gained from the teachings of my parents as well as leaders and teachers at minority institutions.

The positive impact that HBCUs have on their students, faculty, and alumni has been documented over the years in various ways. A 2015 Gallup poll shows that:

> Black graduates of HBCUs are more likely than Black graduates of other institutions to be thriving—strong, consistent and progressing—in a number of areas of their lives, particularly in their financial and purpose well-being. The thriving gap between Black graduates of HBCUs and Black graduates of other schools is the largest in financial well-being, which gauges how effectively people are managing their economic lives to reduce stress and increase security. Four in 10 Black HBCU graduates (40%) are thriving in this area, compared with fewer than three in 10 (29%) Black graduates of other schools.[1]

According to the results of the survey, 55 percent of Black HBCU graduates "strongly agreed" that their college or university "prepared them well for life outside of college," compared to less than 30 percent of non-HBCU Black graduates. About half of Black HBCU graduates said their college or university was "the perfect school" for them, compared to 34 percent of non-HBCU Black alumni. Nearly half also said they couldn't "imagine a world" without the HBCU they attended. Only 25 percent of Black graduates of predominantly White institutions agreed.[2] So contrary to the belief of many, Black graduates of HBCUs fare quite well in life. When it comes to graduating Black students and preparing them for impactful, successful careers, HBCUs play an integral role. HBCUs are indispensable to many Black students and their communities.

Graduates of HBCUs make huge contributions to our society. Although there are only 107 HBCUs as compared to over 4,000 universities nationwide, they make a significant impact on society. While HBCUs make up only 3 percent of the country's colleges and universities, they produce close to 20 percent of all Black college graduates. When it comes to science, technology, engineering, and math (STEM) education, 25 percent of Black graduates' STEM degrees are earned at HBCUs. The majority of Black teachers, physicians, and lawyers earn their undergraduate degrees from HBCUs.[3] Many individuals who have risen to fame and notoriety for their career successes attended HBCUs. These include Vice President of the United States Kamala Harris, Congressman John Lewis, Dr. Booker T. Washington, Dr. Martin Luther King, Jr., Oprah Winfrey, Herman Cain, Toni Morrison, Ruth Carter, Wanda Sykes, Spike Lee, and Michael Strahan, to name a few.

While many within the HBCU communities recognize their importance and impact, many outside of the community do not. Many are unaware that HBCUs annually have a $14.8 billion national economic impact, as well as 134,090 jobs for their local and regional economies altogether.[4] In other words, HBCUs work not only for the benefit of their students, but also for the good of their communities and country as a whole.

All HBCUs were founded for the purpose of educating Blacks. The foundation of most was built upon the concept of preparing these students to enter the workforce, contribute to their communities and serve as mentors and role models to others. The majority of HBCUs set themselves apart from majority institutions because they provide their students with a nurturing environment and individualized attention that they might not otherwise receive. They provide a place to grow and mature. Most of them provide a home and safe haven for their students, cultivate their potential, and make them leaders.

The professors at HBCUs tend to be more opinionated, caring and concerned about their students and their educational journeys. Although this kind of attention is not always initially well received, many alumni express their appreciation later in life as they mature, marry, and have children of their own. As an example, I have a whole file of correspondence from alumni of Hampton approximately fifteen to twenty years after graduation who say that they detested many of the rules in our Dress Code such as wearing business attire when interviewing for jobs or internships; wearing dresses and suits to cabarets and formal events; not allowing "doo rags" on campus by the young men; and not allowing the young ladies to wear their dresses and skirts so short that one can see their panties. Now that they are out into the world with children of their own, they say, "Please don't change your policy because I want my son or daughter to attend Hampton."

The interesting thing about Hampton's dress code is that many students and some of the parents of students who were denied admission become major critics of the policy. Just recently, a person who identified herself as a parent wrote and accused the University of being anti-Black because our dress code was out of the mainstream of "Blackness." She said that she would put her concerns on social media. Our vice president who has responsibility for student personnel responded, . . . "Although HBCUs are not a monolith, the ones that I am familiar with have values, standards, rules and regulations that set them apart from some of the majority institutions."

Based on my leadership experiences at HBCUs, I have seen the positive impact of caring professors and administrators on students firsthand. I have heard the stories. I have seen the results. I have directly benefited from their impact. It is my belief that the concepts and practices that make the HBCU experience special and their graduates successful can be applied universally, no matter the type of institution. Therefore, this book is designed to offer advice as to what promulgates student success in college.

Perhaps there has never been a time in our history when this kind of information and advice was more timely. I say that in addition to "normal" kinds of uncertainties and distress that are associated with young adults such as maturation issues, finances, new environments, new people, male/female conflicts, bullying, and misinformation brought on by social media, students are facing depression and other mental challenges due to the COVID-19 pandemic. Their uneasiness is understandable because as of March 2021, the coronavirus had been responsible for over 120 million cases with over 2.55 million deaths worldwide. In the United States alone, there have been over 500,000 deaths. Think about it, witnessing increased hospitalizations and deaths of family, friends, neighbors, teachers, coaches, and others related to COVID-19, is cause for additional stress.

This book is designed to provide information and guidance both personally and educationally to students who are interested in attending college, those already in college, and to parents who desire to see their children succeed. It cannot be overstated the influence (good or bad) that parents have on their children. In these chapters, I have provided information related to desirable life skills and advice for students and parents about necessary preparations for college; parental responsibilities; history and opportunities of federal college financing; expectations once matriculation begins; skills necessary to succeed in college and life; and examples of institutional offerings, including the prioritizing of mental health support.

In preparing students for college, the book discusses such necessities as completing the Free Application for Federal Student Aid (FAFSA), the requirement for medical clearances, as well as suggested items of clothing. Parents are asked to model and promote good character development, a strong work ethic, and service to others. Financing a college education is discussed in detail with an emphasis on personal savings; individual state 529 Plans; corporate scholarships; federal student aid programs; and corporate relief plans. Other topics deal with the college experience itself and the positive values that most, if not all, institutions of higher education provide.

I also share with readers my thoughts on desired personal behavior for young college-age students, including abstaining from drugs. My advice is grounded in the twelve personal principles below that will assist anyone—young or old—in succeeding in any venue. They have served me well, and, hopefully, they will be helpful to others.

HARVEY'S PRINCIPLES OF SUCCESS

1. Never compromise the character traits of honesty, integrity, respect, trust, and responsible personal behavior.
2. There is no substitute for hard work.
3. Be of service to others if possible.
4. Have a moral compass.
5. Set your goals high and dream no small dreams.
6. Be competitive and never give up.
7. Say NO to distractions.
8. Do not sit back and wish for something positive to happen in your life. Endeavor to make it happen.
9. You cannot finish a race if you do not start it.

10. Do not allow anyone to steal your joy.
11. Be significant in all undertakings.
12. Believe in yourself.

The above principles are not all-encompassing, but they will go a long way toward personal success and happiness. In the past, older adults actually taught young people the means of achieving personal success, motivated them to set high standards, and inspired them to adopt first-class values. Unfortunately, this guidance is not as prevalent today. We need these kinds of role models again in our communities. We need the teachers, preachers, neighbors, coaches, community leaders, and others to stress to this generation of young people the importance of first-class values and character. Many have been led to believe that high-class standards of behavior are reserved for a privileged few. This is utter nonsense as students and others from low-income and first-generation families can do and achieve anything that anyone else can. Promoting high-class standards and first-class values are about people caring about other people and wanting a better world for everyone.

Many of the younger generation say that they get tired of hearing how things used to be "back in the old days." They should listen because everyone would be better off if we would return to the times when standards of appearance, behavior, and civility in our society really mattered. I believe that if we would embrace some of those old-fashioned values and standards that were practiced in the past, our world would be different and better. We are challenged because too many of us have abandoned the basic idea of conforming to good and proper behavior. Parents allow their children to dress and behave in any manner that they wish; they allow them to address their elders with little or no respect; and to top it all off, few are rarely held accountable for their behavior. Parents have an obligation to be decent and respectful human beings and to lead by example in teaching their children to act in the same manner.

America was built on diverse views. Unfortunately, our society is polarized more today than ever before. This polarization, fueled by the partisan divide between politicians and some in the media, has produced the highest levels of incivility that the country has ever witnessed. Social media is no better as it too has become a tool of division.

Parents particularly, but other adults in our neighborhoods and communities, should take it upon themselves to correct and change the trajectory that some of our young people are on. We should not be afraid to tell young people the difference between right and wrong as it relates to their appearance, language, attitude, and behavior. Parents also should not be discouraged by criticism from others when they are trying to get their children to be decent human beings with certain values and standards.

All of us have to do a better job of looking out for each other by teaching values and principles of decency. If parents and teachers are trying to be peers instead of role models, we are headed down the wrong path. Children should try to emulate parents and teachers, not the other way around. Trying to maintain the same fashion and social trends of their children are not the standards that should be set by parents in our society today. Unfortunately, it is happening more frequently as of late and it is detrimental to our young people. Parents should not try to be their children's Best Friends for Life (BFF) or "BESTIE." Parents need to realize that wonderful relationships can be had with their children without having to look, dress, or talk like them. It is parents' responsibility and duty to establish the path that their children should follow. Parents cannot lead if they are walking behind them. Think about it.

It is my hope that this book will provide students with a blueprint for success in college. By developing a good work ethic and learning an appropriate skill set, along with embracing such personal traits as honesty, integrity, respect, loyalty, and confidence, there is no doubt in my mind that they will achieve sustainable success in life.

CHAPTER II

PREPARING FOR COLLEGE

INTRODUCING THE COLLEGE CONCEPT

Many people believe that college preparation begins with the first day of high school. This could not be further from the truth. College preparation should actually begin much earlier in a child's life. Some believe that middle school is the appropriate time to expose students to college, but I believe that young children should be exposed to the concept of attending college as early as elementary school. This exposure can be increased and nurtured as children mature and progress in school.

Typically, elementary students are excited about school. What better time than this to capture their attention, encourage their love of learning, and promote college as a part of their future? Teachers are on the frontlines in classrooms. They know all too well the importance of attending college. Had they not attended, they would not have been able to enter the teaching profession. With a captive audience of young minds who are often enthralled with their teachers, elementary school teachers can help begin the preparation process for young students by planting the college seed in their minds as a goal and expectation for their futures.

Individual classroom teachers can promote college to their students, but the entire school can participate as well by posting and displaying college paraphernalia on bulletin boards and other display areas in the building. My office often receives letters and calls from teachers, counselors, and principals requesting Hampton University items to display to assist them in promoting a college education to their students. Of course, we willingly send posters, pennants, pencils, pens, and other items that can be used and displayed in the schools.

Contrary to what some believe, that preparation does not only take place in the classroom; it also takes place in the home and in the community. Parents can begin early by talking to their young children about college. Children are often asked by parents, "What do you want to be when you grow up?" When children answer, parents can share with them how education, specifically attending college, is a big step in the process of reaching their goals. In addition, parents who have attended college should talk to their children about their college experiences and how those experiences impacted their lives. They can even take children to visit the college they attended or others, as well as allow them to attend sporting and other events and activities on a college campus. This exposes the young children to college early, and they begin to see it as a part of their journey in life.

Young children look forward to being able to do certain things when they get older. You often hear them say, "When I turn 10, I can . . ." or "When I get to high school, I want to . . ." or "For my sixteenth birthday, I am going to . . ." Why not add, "When I go to college . . ." to those conversations. Make college something that they look forward to and view as an expectation. Research has shown that children often perform to the level that is expected of them. If it is made known to them early that they are expected to attend college, their performance throughout their educational journey will likely reflect that expectation.

I am sure that you are wondering when I will begin to talk about academics. You are probably wondering this because most people associate college preparation and success with academic preparation and success. Of course, academics are a major part of the college experience, but there are numerous stories of individuals with great mental aptitude and outstanding grades who were not successful in college. This is because preparation for college involves a lot more than grades and courses. Before we delve into the obvious, I will discuss some other areas that are important to college preparation and why.

SOCIAL/CIVIC/COMMUNITY ENGAGEMENT

Social/civic/community involvement is an area that I believe to be important to college preparation. In college, students are exposed to people with diverse ethnic, racial, cultural, religious, ideological, socioeconomic, regional, family, and other backgrounds. In the college environment, students are expected to appreciate and respect these differences. They are also expected to work together in class, participate in group activities, socialize, and share common spaces. Students who have lived sheltered lives and have not been exposed to individuals outside of their small circle or who have not been involved in clubs and organizations often find this difficult and do not interact well with peers who may be in some way different from them.

Getting students involved in activities before they go to college is one way of preparing them for college. This too can begin early in life. Organizations such as Boys Scouts, Girl Scouts, 4-H Clubs, as well as Jack and Jill of America, provide young people exposure to others and teach them about leadership, problem-solving, effective communication, responsibility, and teamwork on projects and goals. Being a part of such groups helps students learn how to work with others to develop ideas and move an idea from a concept to a completed project. Along the way, they learn how to disagree diplomatically, how to accept criticism and learn from it, as well as how to compromise and work together for the greater good. All of this builds character.

In addition, organized team sports are also a good way of preparing students for college. There are numerous community football, basketball, track, soccer, lacrosse, and other sports teams that students can participate in outside of the school. Being involved in sports emphasizes the importance of teamwork, conditioning of the mind and body, relationships, time management, responsibility, setting of goals, and leadership. Students learn that they cannot win by focusing just on themselves as they are just one piece of the puzzle. While it is important for them to be prepared as individual athletes, they must work together with their coaches and fellow teammates in order to be successful. Participating in sports and other activities outside of school broadens students' interactions with those with whom they might not otherwise have contact, such as students who live in different neighborhoods and have differing experiences.

Extracurricular school activities are important as well. Interacting with peers and teachers outside of the classroom also gives students a different social experience. These activities are more plentiful at the middle school and high school levels. Some common activities in such organizations as the National Honor Society, Key Club, Student Council, JROTC, cheerleading, sports, and others can be found in most schools. However, there are other organizations, such as the drama and music clubs, and mentoring groups, in which students can also get involved. I encourage all students to join at least two organizations, one school-based and one community-based, so that they will have an opportunity to learn and grow from and with others.

The concepts of leadership, teamwork, and effective communication that participation in organizations and activities provide are extremely important to college success. Why not expose students to these concepts and engage them early in activities that promote such, so that they become a part of them? If this is done, students will likely be better prepared for success in college. Many colleges even use participation in extracurricular activities as criterion for admission. Participating in such activities would serve students well.

MENTORSHIP

Another aspect of being successful in college is having a good support team. Learning is not something that should always be done in isolation. Yes, there is much that you can learn on your own, but there is even more that you can learn from others. Throughout my life, I understood the importance of mentoring. As a result, I have had several mentors throughout my career as well as served as a mentor to many others. My mentorship afforded eighteen members of my administrative team at Hampton to become presidents and CEOs of colleges, universities, and other organizations.

Most students have support from family and friends, but I believe having mentors is also important. A mentor is a person who provides advice and guidance on various matters. It is common for individuals to have multiple mentors, each with a specific purpose. One mentor may provide educational or career guidance; another might offer personal or professional advice. Then there are those mentors who give valuable input to every aspect of one's life. Students should not wait to seek out mentors once they arrive to college. Mentors can help them prepare for college as well as support them once they arrive.

Mentors can come from all walks of life. They do not have to just come from leaders in the community, churches, or organizations. They may be a neighbor, friend, mail carrier, janitor, teacher, or others. They must, however, be genuine, sincere, and worthy, having the mentee's best interest in mind.

In any mentoring relationship, asking questions is important. Mentors should ask questions of their mentees and mentees should ask questions of their mentors so that there is a clear understanding between them. Questioning is a sure method for obtaining pertinent information and it helps to direct the thinking of both the person asking the questions and those providing the answers to the questions. Possessing an inquisitive mind and persona enhances intellectual development and is an important aspect of life-long learning.

All of my life I have asked many questions, both professionally and personally. Answers to questions allow me to learn more as well as get a measure of the depth and trustworthiness of the individual responding. A positive occurrence has taken place if the response to a question is open, honest, and forthright. If, on the other hand, the response is disingenuous, unduly emotional, and not fully forthcoming, then a negative occurrence has transpired. I encourage everyone to always be truthful when responding to questions. As mentioned earlier, honesty is important.

The leading authority on leadership, John C. Maxwell, in his book *Good Leaders Ask Great Questions*, states unequivocally, "If you want to be successful and reach your leadership potential, you need to embrace asking questions as a lifestyle."[1] Some of his other thoughts on the art and value of questioning are:

> If you want answers, you must ask questions.
> Questions unlock and open doors that otherwise remain closed.
> Successful leaders relentlessly ask questions . . .
> The most effective way to connect with others is by asking questions.
> Questions cultivate humility.[2]

Maxwell's comments on the cultivation of humility are profound. They demonstrate again to me what an extraordinary leader and teacher he is. For example, he says, "When I began to be honest with myself, allow my weakness to humble me, and go to God for help, I began to change. I became more open and authentic. I was willing to admit my mistakes and weaknesses. I developed appropriate humility, and I began to change and grow." He ponders, ". . .Isn't it strange how we must surrender being right in order to find what's right, how humility enables us to be authentic, vulnerable, trustworthy, and intimate with others? People are open to those who are open to them."[3]

My relationships with my mentors were always open and honest. I am thankful that I took the time to ask questions of and listen to all of them. Had I not, I may not have made the decisions that led me down the right paths personally and professionally. Listening is truly an important aspect of the mentor/mentee relationship. I encourage each of you to identify and establish relationships with personal and professional mentors. If you have mentors, and it has been a while since you spoke with them, take the time to reach out. Remember, you are never too old to learn something new. All you have to do is be willing to listen.

My parents were my first mentors and role models, but there were others. In junior and senior high school, I still remember the names of teachers who guided me in an extraordinary way. One was Mrs. Rheutelia Andrews who was secretary to the director and a typing instructor. She gave me some advice that I still use today. In her twelfth grade typing class, I was the fastest typist among both females and males in my class. Many in my class, including Mrs. Andrews, were surprised that I could type as fast as I did, even though I had never had any kind of typing training. Once it became clear that the typing test that I had excelled at was no fluke, Mrs. Andrews called me into her office one day and then gave me this advice. She said, "You are currently typing 68 correct words per minute and that is faster than anyone else in the class. I want you to know that you have a talent that quite frankly is usually reserved for females." She said, "I'd like for you to always aim high with your goals in everything that you do. Do not allow anyone to pigeonhole you into an inferior category. Specifically, no matter what you do, be the very best at it. It makes no difference if your competition is a male or female, black or white, old or young. Understand that you have gifts which will cause you to excel."

My parents had emphasized similar opinions to me on many occasions. Specifically, they had talked about the fact that if others had excelled at any task, then my sister Anne and I could excel also. My dad used to remind us of the quote that you are only inferior at your own consent. My parents and Mrs. Andrews' words continue to serve as a guide and I am also highly appreciative for them. Her words remind me of a speech that Dr. Martin Luther King, Jr. made in Philadelphia, Pennsylvania, on October 26, 1967, at Barratt Jr. High School.

> If it falls your lot to be a street sweeper
> Sweep streets like Michelangelo painted pictures;
> Sweep streets like Beethoven composed music;
> Sweep streets like Leontyne Price sings before the
>   Metropolitan Opera;
> Sweep streets like Shakespeare wrote poetry;
> Sweep streets so well that all of the hosts of heaven and earth
> will have to pause and say;
> Here lived a great street sweeper who swept his job well.
> If you can't be a pine at the top of the hill, be a shrub in the
>   valley.
> Be the best little shrub on the side of the hill. [4]

Another individual who had a lasting impact on me was Mr. S. C. Cheatham. Although he was the owner and director of a local funeral home, he also served as the high school football coach. Coach Cheatham emphasized that in order to be successful in football and in life, there were four fundamental steps that we should follow. The first step was understanding the importance of conditioning the mind and the body. Second, he insisted that we develop and set goals on a daily basis. This included goals for us to aspire to in practice as well as in games. Third, he said that an individual must have a clear strategy for achieving those goals. Fourth, he stressed the importance of teamwork. I can hear him now saying that "There is not an 'I' in team." He emphasized that all of us must work together to achieve desired results. Coach Cheatham said that if we were to adhere to these four principles, they would go a long way toward making us successful. His teachings were correct then and they are correct now.

Middle and high school students usually seek out teachers, counselors, coaches, or adults within their community whom they admire to serve as their mentors. These mentors help guide students in making choices and decisions that affect their futures. They are there to offer advice, give direction, and sometimes, just to listen. It is good for mentors to spend personal one-on-one time with their mentees to develop a relationship that is built upon honesty and trust, so that students are confident that the mentor is genuinely concerned about them.

As students matriculate in college and journey through life, they will gain other mentors along the way. These mentor relationships will be discussed further in the chapter on "Valuing the College Community."

ACADEMIC PREPARATION

Now, we will discuss academic preparation for college. It is never too early to begin looking at the college admission requirements for schools that students are interested in attending. These requirements will help students choose the appropriate classes to enroll in while in middle and high school. While high school transcripts, not middle school transcripts, are often required for college admission, the courses completed in middle school should be considered preparation for the high school courses to be successfully completed. With this in mind, students should attempt to take classes that fit the college preparatory track to make sure that they have the knowledge and skills necessary for college admission.

I believe that students should pursue the most rigorous program of study available. This means taking dual enrollment classes, honors, Advanced Placement (AP), and other challenging courses. Some middle and high schools offer career tracks, academies, and other unique ways of providing students not only with the content they need for college admission, but also content that is specific to career fields. For example, students may take AP classes in high school or dual enrollment with colleges that introduce them to the fields of engineering, health sciences, technology, education, entrepreneurship, and law. When AP or dual enrollment courses are available, students should take advantage, for this enables them to get an early feel for a given career. They may discover that they have made the right choice or they may decide that another career might suit them better. Having this exposure early on will likely help them decide on a career prior to college and decrease the likelihood of them changing majors and career goals because they were not aware of all of the requirements their choice entailed.

The high school transcript is a guide for college admission as it gives colleges a good idea of just how academically prepared a student is for college. I use the term "good idea" because the transcript is a powerful indicator of college success, but it is not absolute. There have been students with outstanding high school transcripts and grade point averages who were not successful in college and those with not so great transcripts who performed exceptionally well in college. In some cases, students with great transcripts were enrolled in courses that were not very rigorous. Therefore, when they arrived at college they could not handle the workload and expectations. On the other hand, students with transcripts which were not the best were successful because they were accustomed to rigorous courses and possessed the skills necessary for success in college classes.

At Hampton, we have a practice of admitting a small group of students annually who do not meet our normal admission requirements.

We reserve a small percentage of the spaces in our freshman class for students in this category. Over the years, we have tracked the progress of these students to determine their success in college. What we have discovered is that by the senior year, this group of students performs at the same level as the students who met the standard admission requirements. The gap between them slowly diminished as they studied, interacted, and engaged in the academic environment. By their senior year, the percentage is approximately the same for those in both groups as it relates to their academics as well as punishment for misbehaving.

Not many schools have such a practice so there are many students who are not admitted into college because their transcripts do not meet normal admission requirements. With this in mind, I encourage any student who is interested in attending college to make their academics a priority, especially in high school.

Everything counts when it comes to the courses you take and the grades you make in high school. It is imperative for students who plan to attend college to enroll in the appropriate classes, focus on their studies, make sound personal decisions, develop good study skills, and make good grades.

Using college admission criteria as a guide, students should plan their high school class schedules early. Nothing is wrong with planning for all four years of high school in the ninth grade. It may become necessary to change the plan along the way, but having a plan early on is beneficial. Colleges require a certain number of courses in English, math, social studies, foreign language, and science as basic criteria. Beyond that, college admission policies vary from school to school. Many of the other courses required for college admission and graduation are electives. These elective courses should be chosen wisely. They should be chosen based on high school graduation requirements, college admission requirements, and student interests.

During their high school days, students should expand their reading and writing activities and get into the habit of spending more time completing homework. They should also attempt to engage and interact with teachers as frequently as possible.

In many instances, high school students have opportunities to earn college credit while still in high school. As mentioned earlier, two programs that make this possible are the AP and dual enrollment programs. Advanced Placement courses allow students to enroll in more rigorous courses in several fields of study, including the arts, English, history, social sciences, science, math, and computer science, as well as world languages and culture. At the end of the course, students can take a standardized AP Exam and with the required score, receive college credit for the course. Students also have opportunities to enroll in college courses while still in high school and earn course credit for high school and college. Many take advantage of these programs and already have college credit when they enter as freshmen. This too is another way of getting prepared for college before you actually arrive.

Good study habits and skills can be very useful throughout your educational career. These too should be developed and utilized early. In order to be successful in school, it is important to study. You should discipline yourself and allow time for study on a regular basis. Some of you might ask, "What if I do well without studying?" My answer would be, "Imagine how much better you would do if you DID study." Studying helps to retain information and encourages balance, structure, and organization. Those who set aside time to study tend to be better students than those who do not.

When you go to college, you will face a new set of courses, new teachers and approaches to teaching, as well as a new way of life. It is important to be able to read and study for all of your classes as well as balance your extracurricular/social activities. Having good reading and study habits prior to coming to college makes this transition less difficult. Good reading habits are important and will be beneficial all of your life!

COLLEGE SELECTION PROCESS

All of the recommendations that I have given thus far lead to choosing a college that is right for you. In attempting to reach this goal, I suggest the following steps. The first step is to conduct your research about the colleges that you have an interest in attending. Seek assistance from counselors, family, friends, websites, and students who already attend the institution that you have an interest in attending. Ask pertinent and relevant questions as they relate to your needs and desires. Seek accurate information, not just limited, marketing intelligence. Limit your use of social media when seeking accurate information about an institution because the information provided may not be accurate. As you do your research, establish realistic enrollment options. Think about your fit within each institution, your academic goals, your finances, and your future.

The next step is to arrange college visits. This can be done in the summer, spring break, holidays, or with an organized college tour. Maximize this opportunity by being inquisitive with your tour guide. A college visit may be one of the most important factors that you will use when narrowing your choices. Ask about rules, regulations, codes of conduct, honors programs, and dress. Try and ascertain if you are a fit for the institution. This is important because if you are not a good fit, you are inviting trouble for yourself.

Remember: Do your research. Ask questions. For example, thorough research and asking questions about all facets of college offerings are extremely important. Aside from the obvious questions about academics, there are other important areas as well. Case in point, if the institution offers remote instruction, does it offer remote services? It should not be left to the student alone to cope with and overcome adversities related to academics, mental health, social interactions, or personal matters. Students should ask a series of questions during these tumultuous times: Does the university have a framework for health and wellness? Are there mental health services to address stress management, anxiety, depression, trauma, and healthy personal relationships? If you are a remote learner in another country, what means are available for you to stay connected and to interact with friends and acquaintances? Does the institution promote ample opportunities for students to connect socially?

What about things such as opportunities for students to connect socially? An institution should not downplay the prioritization of interacting socially with students who are away from the campus.

A college or university should be prepared to equip students on some of these topics before a crisis occurs. Being prepared for these types of situations are some of the ways in which a first-rate university assists its students beyond the classroom.

As with most things, planning should be a part of this decision-making process. Identify colleges that you are fairly certain will accept you. Next, identify those that you feel may or may not accept you. Last, identify those that you do not believe will provide a favorable response. You may be surprised at the results. Admission committees are composed of individuals who may not have bias, but do have special interests. There are a number of examples that I have used in making this point. Suppose your grades and test scores do not meet normal admission requirements, but you have won multiple singing contests, or you are an avid mountain climber, or chess champion, or have written several children's books. One or more of these talents may pique the interest of one or more of the admissions committee members. Therefore, they become an advocate for you with others on the committee.

FINANCIAL PREPARATION

An obviously important aspect of preparing for college is identifying the money to help pay for the higher education experience. In the chapter on financing for college, I go into detail on my thoughts about parental, federal, and institutional responsibilities and opportunities. This analysis includes an historical overview of some of the programs and other aspects regarding college financing. There are things, however, that students, parents, and guardians should do as they prepare for college.

Remember that paying for college rests first with your family. In a 2020 study entitled, "How America Pays for College," Sallie Mae found that the typical American household paid 44 percent of their child's higher education expenses. The breakdown of other support was 25 percent scholarships and grants, 21 percent borrowing, and 1 percent friends and family.[5]

Despite these statistics, many folks today are seeking or proposing a free ride. This is not realistic. Therefore, the serious student should explore federal, state, and institutional aid in addition to family support. This starts with the completion of a document called FAFSA (Free Application for Federal Student Aid). Every student should complete a FAFSA because the form is not only used to determine federal support, but is used by many states, as well as colleges and universities, to determine eligibility for aid. In doing so, you are applying for aid not only from the federal government, but from state and higher educational institutions as well. Although every state institution does not require a FAFSA, the vast majority utilize the information as a guide for the disbursement of their aid.

It is important to note that irrespective of family income or age, any student can receive some form of federal aid to attend an eligible college, technical school, vocational school, or graduate school as long as certain criteria are met. For that reason, extreme care should be taken in completing the application. According to the U.S. Department of Education, some of the general eligibility requirements for receiving federal aid are listed below:

1. Demonstrate financial need (for most programs);
2. Be a US citizen or an eligible noncitizen;
3. Have a valid Social Security number;
4. Be registered with Selective Service if you're a male between the ages of eighteen and twenty-five;
5. Be enrolled or accepted for enrollment in an eligible degree or certificate program;
6. Be enrolled at least half-time (for most programs);
7. Maintain satisfactory academic progress in college, career school, or graduate school;
8. Sign the certification statement on the Free Application for Federal Student Aid (FAFSA) form stating that
   ▶ You are not in default on a federal student loan and do not owe money on a federal grant, and
   ▶ You will use federal student aid only for educational purposes; and
9. Show you're qualified to obtain a college or career school education by
   ▶ Having a high school diploma or a General Educational Development (GED) certificate or a state-recognized equivalent; or

- ► Completing a high school education in a home school setting approved under state law; or
- ► In an eligible career pathways programs.[6]

You may have heard some say that the FAFSA form is difficult to complete. A lot of the complaints seem to be unwarranted and unfortunately may be more generational. Accurately completing the FAFSA is the doorway to receiving financial assistance to help college-bound students achieve their goals and gain expertise in a field of study, which may end up being their life's work. Along with their parents, guardians, or others to assist, students should take the necessary time to do a thorough job on this application. Some of the mistakes that are made are relatively simple ones, and extreme care should be taken to avoid these errors. The National Association of Financial Aid Administrators has identified the more common errors or mistakes as not filling in all of the blanks, using inaccurate social security numbers and addresses, misrepresenting marital status, not listing the college to be attended, and failing to sign and date the form.[7]

Once the decision is made regarding the college to attend, and the finances arranged, let's review some of the necessities that will aid in the transition. Medical clearances and applications for housing must be completed. Relevant policies such as the Official Student Handbook, Code of Conduct, Dress Codes, and dormitory curfews (if any) must be known and understood. A packing list of personal items might prove helpful as well.

All of the approximately 4,000 higher educational institutions in the country do not require the same information or have the same policies. Most, however, have official requirements to assist new students and promulgate the standards and values of that particular institution. To give an example and provide a guide for new students at any institution in the country, listed below are some of the policies and requirements that Hampton University follows. Any student, no matter what college or university they choose to attend, may use this information as a guide and checklist for any aspect that may be applicable to them.

For obvious reasons, a medical clearance is mandatory at all institutions of higher education. Immunizations and vaccinations are required to protect the students and the community at large. The Centers for Disease Control (CDC) has guidelines that most first-rate institutions follow relating to MMR (measles, mumps, and rubella), Tdap (tetanus, diphtheria, and pertussis), and Meningococcal shots. Additionally, Hampton University requires a Hepatitis "A" vaccination and a COVID-19 vaccine. The University strongly recommends Hepatitis "B" vaccinations and an annual influenza (flu) shot. Hampton also requires students with chronic illnesses to register with the Office of Disability Services and establish care at the institution's health center in the event that referrals to specialists are required.

As of late, mental health has begun to receive more scrutiny. More and more students are coming to college in a state of anxiety and depression. If this is the case, these students should be encouraged to seek the services of their respective Student Counseling Center, or participate in group therapy, weekly yoga, or exercise classes. Involvement in other campus events have proven to be a source of support for good mental health and well-being. The institution's health center can also provide referrals to local psychiatrists or psychologists.

To assist students with their medical clearances, they should schedule an appointment with their health-care provider for a physical examination and completion of required documents before their arrival on campus. Any and all required medical documents should also be taken to their physician for completion. The physician should sign and date all of the forms. Medical clearances are a necessary and important step for your matriculation. Make sure that this step is treated as such.

OTHER IMPORTANT INFORMATION

While preparing to leave home for college, think about needed items to take with you. For example, clothes and shoes should be discussed with parents and guardians because it is unlikely that the relatively small dormitory rooms will be able to accommodate all of the wardrobe that you and your roommate possess. After discussing this with colleagues and students, I am outlining the minimum basic attire for females and males.

For females, an appropriate business length dark skirted suit; white blouse; hosiery; several pairs of jeans plus other pants; approximately five different skirts and blouses; two or three pairs of comfortable dress shoes; two or three pairs of casual shoes; a couple pair of tennis and shower shoes; and enough underwear for at least two weeks.

For men, my suggestions are a blue blazer and another sport coat or suit; several pairs of jeans plus other pants; at least two white shirts and ties; a black and tan pair of dress shoes; two or three pairs of casual shoes; at least three pairs of sneakers and a pair of shower shoes; and at least two weeks of underwear.

In addition to clothes, both males and females should develop a packing list of items that could prove helpful to them. Each student is different, with a different set of financial circumstances, but the list below is provided for consideration.

Suggested items:

1. Medication—especially for colds/flu/congestion
2. Laptop or tablet
3. Printer
4. Iron
5. Clock/radio
6. Clothes hangers and dirty clothes hamper
7. Dictionary and thesaurus
8. Towels/soap and other toiletries
9. Laundry detergent
10. Footlocker that locks
11. Broom, dustpan, small waste basket, and trash bags
12. Bedspreads and bed liners

Some of the prohibited items at a number of colleges are portable air conditioners; microwave and toaster ovens; cooking appliances of any kind (fire hazards); alcohol and illegal drugs (marijuana is illegal in some states); guns; fireworks or incendiary devices; and weapons of any type, including knives. Some colleges allow some of the above items. Therefore, be sure to do your research before coming on a campus that does not permit some of them.

I mentioned earlier that all institutions do not have the same set of guidelines, procedures, and policies. Practically all have their own values and standards, however. In order to give an example of the values of one university that obviously I am familiar with, listed below is the official Code of Conduct for Hampton University.

Code of Conduct

Joining the Hampton Family is an honor and requires each individual to uphold the policies, regulations, and guidelines established for students, faculty, administration, professional and other employees, and the laws of the Commonwealth of Virginia. Members of the Hampton Family embrace the core values of Exceptional Character: Respect, Professionalism, Integrity, and Community. No member shall lie, cheat or steal and each member is required to adhere to and conform to the instructions and guidance of the leadership of his/her respective area. Therefore, in maintaining The Standard of Excellence, the following are expected of each member of the Hampton Family:

Respect:

1. **To respect himself or herself.**

   Each member of the Hampton Family will exhibit a high degree of maturity and self-respect and foster an appreciation for other cultures, one's own cultural background, as well as the cultural heritage from which Hampton University was born. It is only through these appreciations that the future of our university can be sustained indefinitely.

2. **To respect the dignity, feelings, worth, and values of others.**

   Each member of the Hampton Family will respect one another and visitors as if they were guests in one's home. Students, faculty, and staff should engage in behaviors that are uplifting and encouraging. Moreover, to accost, bully, cajole, or proselytize students, faculty or staff, parents or others, use vile, obscene or abusive language or exhibit lewd behavior, is in direct violation of the Hampton University Code, on or off campus.

Professionalism:

3. **To foster a personal professional work ethic within the Hampton University Family.**

   Every member of the Hampton Family must strive for efficiency and job perfection. Each individual must exhibit a commitment to serve, and tasks must be executed in a humane and civil manner.

4. **To foster an open, fair, and caring environment.**

   The University will maintain an open and caring environment. It is understood that intellectual stimulation is nurtured through the sharing of ideas. In cases where issues arise, each member of the Hampton Family is assured equal and fair treatment.

Integrity:

5. **To respect the rights and property of others.**

   Each member of the Hampton Family will only engage in activities that are legal and ethical, both on and off campus. No member shall lie, cheat or steal. Other transgressions include, but are not limited to, harassment of any form, possession of weapons such as knives and firearms, involvement in possession, use, distribution and sale of illegal drugs, theft, vandalism or hazing. Violators will be subject to all applicable provisions listed in the Faculty Handbook, Personnel Policies Manual for Administrative/ Professional and Nonexempt Employees, the Official Student Handbook, the Hampton University Code, and statutes of the Commonwealth of Virginia.

6. **To practice personal, professional, and academic integrity.**

   Personal, professional, and academic integrity is paramount to the survival and potential of the Hampton Family. Therefore, individuals found in violation of Hampton University's policies against lying, cheating, plagiarism, or stealing are subject to disciplinary action that could possibly include dismissal from the University.

Community:

7. **To promote inclusion, while striving to learn from differences in people, ideas, and opinions.**

   Each member of the Hampton Family will support equal rights and opportunities for all regardless of age, sex, race, sexual orientation, religion, disability, ethnic heritage, socio-economic status, political, social, or other affiliation or disaffiliation.

8. **To promote the ethical use of technology and social media.**

   As a Hampton Family we embrace the digital age. Each member of the Hampton Family is expected to use technology in a responsible and respectful manner. Individuals should utilize their best judgment before posting content and should specifically refrain from cyber bullying or using social media to cheat. Uses of technology or social media posts that violate any of the aforementioned tenets of this Code will subject one to disciplinary action.

9. **To be fully responsible for upholding the Hampton University Code.**

   Each member of the Hampton Family will embrace all tenets of the Code of Conduct, Policies, and the Honor Pledge and is encouraged to report all violators to the appropriate administrator or the Council for Institutional Culture and Values.[8]

In this chapter, I have outlined a number of steps that will aid you in your college planning process. You, with the aid of your parents, counselors, and perhaps others, must decide if the college of your choice, as stated earlier, is a good fit. As an example, you may like the academics, but you do not think that you can abide by the honor code or curfew, or some other policy. Doing your research and asking questions are clearly important steps.

SELECTING A MAJOR

Research into major fields of concentration to understand what kind of careers will be pursued must also be considered. You should ask yourself several questions: What subjects do I like? What subjects am I good in? What subjects will advance my career goals? Does the institution of my choice have a good program and reputation in that field? What are the salaries in the fields of study that have piqued my interest?

Although there are other criteria for selecting a college and major field of concentration, salaries seem to garner the most attention. In that regard, let's take a look at some of the highest and lowest paying salaries of college graduates entering the workforce. There are several organizations, including universities, that have analyzed the data and I provide two examples below. Their conclusions differ slightly because the timelines and methodology may be different. The first example is taken from Georgetown University Center on Education and the Workforce analysis of U.S. Census Bureau data. This first chart shows median salaries by major for entry level graduates ages twenty-one to twenty-four years old. The second chart depicts the same majors with the addition of teaching and serving for those professionals' ages twenty-five to twenty-nine years old.

Entry Level Bachelor's Degrees[9]

STEM	$43,000
Health	$41,000
Business	$37,000
Career-focused	$30,000
Arts, humanities, and liberal arts	$29,000

Mid-Career Bachelor's Degrees[10]

STEM	$76,000
Business	$67,000
Health	$65,000
All majors	$61,000
Arts, liberal arts, and humanities	$51,000
Teaching and serving	$46,000

The charts above deal with the categories of employment, while the charts below provide the specifics of the highest and lowest paying majors. These are median wages for those individuals ages twenty-five to fifty-nine.

Highest Paying Majors[11]

Petroleum Engineering	$136,000
Pharmacy and Pharmaceutical Sciences and Administration	$113,000
Metallurgical Engineering	$98,000
Mining and Mineral Engineering	$97,000
Chemical Engineering	$96,000
Electrical Engineering	$93,000
Aerospace Engineering	$90,000
Mechanical Engineering	$87,000
Computer Engineering	$87,000
Geological and Geophysical Engineering	$87,000

Lowest Paying Majors[12]

Family and Consumer Sciences	$45,000
Drama and Theater Arts	$45,000
Elementary Education	$43,000
Theology and Religious Vocations	$43,000
Visual and Performing Arts	$42,000
Teacher Education: Multiple Levels	$42,000
Social Work	$42,000
Studio Arts	$42,000
Human Services and Community Organization	$41,000
Early Childhood Education	$39,000

The above information shows that nine out of the top ten high-paying jobs are in the field of engineering. Several other studies have focused on long-term employment and have reached different conclusions. For example, The Chronicle of Higher Education reported that a study done by the Georgetown University Center on Education and the Workforce indicated that forty years after attending college, an individual who was a liberal arts major had a return on investment (ROI) of nearly $200,000 above all other majors. This study, which was published in January 2020, used data from the

U.S. Department of Education's College Scorecard and expanded a November 2019 report entitled "A First Try at ROI: Ranking 4,500 Colleges." The same study revealed that the return on investment for liberal arts majors ten years after enrollment was $62,000 versus $107,000 for all others. Clearly, the longer the lapse time after graduation, the more favorable the ROI was for liberal arts majors compared to other fields of concentration.[13]

Other research reached similar conclusions about earnings. Derek Loosvelt in an article entitled "Do Liberal Arts Majors Earn More in the Long Run?" indicated that lifetime earnings for computer science majors was approximately $3.2 million compared with $3.45 million for philosophy majors and $3.75 million for those who majored in history.[14]

Which study is the accurate one? Because the focus was on different timelines and age groups, one could conclude that all of the research studies were accurate at the time that they were conducted.

There are other surveys that have also analyzed the median salaries for recent graduates ages twenty-five to thirty, along with those in the age group thirty to fifty-five, and reached the same basic conclusions as the above examples. Therefore, as it relates to salaries alone, the facts are that recent graduates in engineering, science, and technology make more money initially after graduating from college than those in liberal arts, social science, and education. By the time that graduates in the liberal arts, social science, and education reach their mid-career (ages fifty-five to sixty), the median salaries have not only caught up, but in some instances, surpassed the professional group. Clearly, there are positives and negatives that can be said for both groups as it relates to salaries alone.

My view and strong recommendation is that one should not choose a college major and subsequent career on salary alone. Salary comparisons are good, but are not the definitive reasons why a young person should attend an institution of higher education. An individual should not enter a field where there is no interest or aptitude. By no means should anyone select a major field of study based solely on salary. I say often that life is about choices and the choice that is made should take into consideration your talents, needs, interests, and happiness. Does anyone really want a job that they hate and view it as a burden to get up and go to work every morning? Will that extra compensation contribute to a life well-lived?

I have seen a number of people who pursued a field of study for reasons other than their interests. Some did it for salaries. Others did it because their parents wanted them to do so. Still others did it because they had not asked enough questions or done enough research on long-term salary comparisons.

No matter the major that is chosen, the vast majority of college graduates will lead a solid middle-class existence. The important thing to remember is to work hard and study hard. Take advantage of the many academic options that will be offered because there are so many things that one can do with a college degree. As examples, an English or history major can, among other things, go to law school after passing the Law School Admission Test (LSAT). A psychology major can enter medical school upon passing the Medical College Admission Test (MCAT). The important thing is to develop and sharpen your skill set for writing, speaking, analyzing, innovating problem-solving, and teamwork. These are the traits that corporations, graduate schools, and governmental agencies are seeking in individuals to include as a part of their organization. Salaries will come if communication skills, productivity, loyalty, preparation, and teamwork are an integral component of your being.

CHAPTER III

PARENTAL GUIDANCE

The enormous positive effect that good parenting has on the growth, development, and success of children cannot be overstated. Some children may not show it growing up, but the vast majority whom I have come into contact with certainly have expressed appreciation for their parents' guidance later in life.

COMMUNICATION

My first piece of advice to parents is that you must communicate to your children, in word and deed, the significance of desirable personal traits and successful professional characteristics. As it relates to personal traits, start by emphasizing the importance of being a decent human being. It does not matter the race, religion, sex, future occupation, marital status, or the like. Decency is a paramount factor in the pursuit of happiness and a good life. I tell college students often that decency is as important as degrees.

I tell them also that the character traits of honesty, truth, integrity, trustworthiness, respect for one's self and others, and responsible personal behavior never go out of style, no matter one's age or circumstances. Good character is always timely and priceless, and is essential to a life well lived. These values should be communicated early and often.

When General Samuel Chapman Armstrong founded Hampton University, he emphasized the building of character. In an address to the students in 1868, he opened his remarks by saying, "I want to speak to you of conduct and character, the relation between them, and relation to their success in life." He went on to say, "Conduct grows out of character; good conduct out of good character, bad conduct out of bad character; deceitful conduct out of deceitful character. Deceitful conduct may deceive men for a while, but it doesn't deceive God. Conduct, grows out of character, just as a tree grows up from the root."[1]

I was taught the importance of character early in life by my parents. My mother was devoted to building character in the lives of her children, other people's children, friends, acquaintances, and family. She felt that honesty was the cornerstone of good character and that we should "treat people like we want to be treated." I have heard it many times since, but I heard it first from my mother when she said, "Always try to do the right thing, even when no one is looking." While I lay no claim to having always done the right thing, I learned early on that character is an integral part of life.

While promoting positive traits, do not shy away from pointing out negative ones such as lying, cheating, and never admitting when mistakes have been made. I know and have known individuals who suffer from such severe psychosis that they tell traceable lies. One of the sad parts about a situation like this is that practically everyone knows that the individuals are lying but them. I'll bet that every reader knows someone like this as well.

Then there are those persons who never admit that they make mistakes. The fact is that everyone at one time or another has made mistakes. I know that I do. When it is known to me that a mistake has been made, I recommend a three-step process to correct it. First, there should be an acknowledgment of the error. Second, an apology should be immediately issued. Third, the one who made the mistake should endeavor not to do it again. Anything short of this is not acceptable.

Parents, you should also understand that wisdom cannot be passed on without communication. This is both verbal and by example. Do not be afraid to tell your children the difference between right and wrong. Instead of engaging in conversations, too many parents attempt to relate by accepting and/or excusing bad behavior; being buddy-buddy and attempting to be contemporary friends with their children; dressing in today's latest teen fashions such as torn jeans; talking in the lingo of the street or current culture; getting body piercings; and going to a parlor for tattoos. Too many parents want to appear "cool" and "hip," with children and their friends, instead of acting in a mature fashion and understanding that they are from a different generation, no matter the age difference. In many instances, the children do not want this kind of relationship and their friends laugh at the parents' behavior.

Talking and guiding kids on the fundamentals of life and living are important but micromanaging every aspect of their lives is counterproductive. Instead of providing appropriate guidance and direction, many overprotective and overly attentive parents (helicopter parents) do more harm than good. Kids need to develop problem-solving skills. How can they learn to solve problems if parents, grandparents, and other well-meaning people intervene in every situation? As President, I receive letters and copies of letters from these helicopter overseers inquiring or complaining about everything from their child needing a tutor; financial aid questions; questioning the grades that their child received; heat issues in their dorm room; why their child was not selected to join a fraternity or sorority; difficulty with a particular professor; and a myriad of other things.

Another advantage of parents' communication directly with their children is that ongoing conversations might help them overcome some of their anxieties. In *The Wall Street Journal* article entitled, "Is Your Child Emotionally Ready for College," Drs. Anthony Rostain and B. Janet Hibbs reported that in a 2018 annual survey of college students, over 85 percent indicated that at one point or another they felt "overwhelmed."[2] Different people put forth a myriad of explanations for these feelings including family instability, hormonal changes, financial concerns, drugs, alcohol, and negative media influences associated with television programs, movies, music videos, and social media which glorify such low-class behavior as lying, cheating, stealing, untrustworthiness, sexual promiscuity, and disrespect for self and others.

It is no wonder then that young people today, mainly starting in their adolescent years, face a number of challenges which can lead to anxiety. Whatever the reason, in many instances, the young people feel disappointed, disillusioned, and overwhelmed. Parents, you should take the time to talk to your children about these kinds of subjects and issues.

Let them know that at one time or another, everyone has had some form of anxiousness, stress, or anxiety. Assure them that others have encountered obstacles and overcome them and they can as well. Be specific about such things as unstable family life. As an example, I saw an interview recently with Will Smith, the TV and movie personality, who said that growing up he witnessed his father punch his mother in the face. He said that was wrong and he did not want his children growing up in that kind of situation. Further, he told his wife, Jada Pinkett Smith, that under no circumstances would he do that or condone that kind of behavior. He said that if their relationship involved cursing at each other, or physical violence, they would have to separate. Good for him!

I wholeheartedly agree with Will Smith on this matter because it is sound reasoning and good advice. I was also pleased to hear a movie icon express himself publicly because his celebrity status might get more young people to understand that it is wrong to exhibit that kind of behavior. It is incumbent upon parents to advise their children that no matter what is viewed on the various media platforms, classless behavior, even exhibited by celebrities, is not a life form that they should attempt to emulate.

The foundational traits of good character are essential to success. Today, we live in a world where there has been a coarsening of our culture. Actions and behaviors that were considered disgraceful in the past are considered appropriate today. There are things that people do today that would have caused them to be ostracized by their peers or fired by their supervisors twenty-five or thirty years ago. Standards and values that used to be held by good people have sadly been lowered by a growing number in today's culture. Nevertheless, those of us who seek to be successful and be an example to others cannot allow ourselves to be steered away from what is right and best.

Examples of bad character are everywhere these days, and they often influence people to make bad choices and practice bad behaviors. However, seeing bad behavior all around you does not mean that the behavior is right or that you should emulate and copy it. There is an option of doing things differently.

I often say that life is a game of choice, not a game of chance. As a result, the choices that people make in their lives determine their level of success. What many do not realize is that their choices are a direct reflection of their character, be it good or bad. Think about the type of character exhibited in the following situations.

1. An applicant chooses to lie on a job application about a criminal past.
2. A student cheats on an examination or intentionally plagiarizes an essay.
3. An attorney steals money from a client.
4. A financial advisor "borrows" a client's money for personal pursuits.
5. An employee speaks to a supervisor in a loud, demanding, and threatening tone and refuses to follow a directive.

I would venture to say, and hope that every reader agrees with my belief, that all of the above choices reflect bad character and jeopardize the offender's path to success.

For instance, the applicant may have gotten the employment with a criminal past, but because of not being honest on the application, he or she is likely NOT to keep the job. The student who cheated or plagiarized, when caught, will receive a lower grade than if the work had been done honestly and may face severe disciplinary action. The attorney who steals money from a client not only demonstrates a lack of character, but also a lack of integrity and more than likely will be disbarred by the particular state's Supreme Court and never allowed to practice law again. The financial advisor who "borrows" a client's money for personal use could face criminal charges.

The employee who is disrespectful to a supervisor will cause confusion in the workplace and likely lose his/her job.

The choices these individuals made, resulting from bad character, can affect their lives forever. Many times people, especially young people, do not think beyond the moment. They do not think of the consequences, which could potentially be a result of the choices that they make. Often, one bad choice can ruin what a person has worked so hard to accomplish. Unfortunately, this has been the case among many young adults who have gone off to college and experienced a new level of freedom.

One example that comes to mind is that of a female college student who became involved in a relationship with a young man who sold illegal drugs. Through her association with him, she was arrested on drug possession charges and sentenced to time in prison. Her college education was cut short by this and her life took an immediate and unexpected turn. She will never redeem the time of the several years she served in prison. Once released, she had to begin her life all over again, this time with a police record following her every step of the way. Eventually, she used this experience as a message for other young college students, encouraging them to be careful of the choices that they make and the friends that they choose.

Do people with good character make bad choices? Of course they do. However, they recognize their bad choices as such and do their best to make better choices in the future. They seek to make their future choices ones that are reflective of their true character.

J. Hanes states, "A good name is seldom regained. When character is gone, one of the richest jewels of life is lost forever."[3] Parents should emphasize good character as well as the importance of vision, work ethic, and service.

VISION

People who understand the importance and value of vision dream big and look inward for confidence, inspiration, and the roadmap to the future. For example, some of our largest corporations have been built from the vision of a single individual or a small group. By establishing Microsoft, Bill Gates and Paul Allen, having envisioned personal interactive computing as the wave of the future, revolutionized human technology and communication. Beginning as an online bookseller, Jeff Bezos' Amazon is now one of the most valuable companies in the world. Sam Walton's vision for his single 5 & 10 store has multiplied into over 11,000 Walmart stores in over twenty-seven countries.[4]

Vision has no color, creed, gender, or income level. Look at John H. Johnson, one of the most successful publishers in US history. His vision was a simple, yet extraordinary one. He started *Ebony* magazine because he believed "that Black Americans needed positive images to fulfill their potential" and "that you have to change images before you can change acts and institutions."[5] *Ebony* is a magazine devoted to making people feel good about who they are and proud of their heritage. Johnson took this positive images idea and founded an empire.

Madam C. J. Walker, born Sarah Breedlove in 1867, was the daughter of ex-slaves who were sharecroppers in Louisiana. Orphaned at seven, married at fourteen, widowed at twenty, she worked as a washer-woman for eighteen years until 1905. Even with this kind of improvised background, she had a vision that would help tens of thousands of women and make her a millionaire. Madam Walker invented an ointment for the treatment of scalp disease, as well as a process for hair grooming for African American women, and built a cosmetics empire.

For me, a vision is an extraordinary thought, dream, or idea that has an outcome, which enhances, in whole or in part, an individual, group, organization, state, region, or nation. According to my definition, all of us can be visionaries. We can all imagine the great possibilities inherent in that nebulous space between the "what is" and the "what can be." Your vision does not have to be as grand or as broad as those I mentioned. It can simply be a vision for your career, family, job, business, church, or community. However, having a vision is important because it serves as a guide for where you want to go in life.

As parents help to prepare their children for adulthood and life, discussions about successful job-related characteristics are also in order. In my judgment, two of the most significant ones are the development of a strong work ethic and being of service to others.

WORK ETHIC

There is no substitute for hard work. Many of us have heard people say, "You sure are lucky." They may be talking about professional achievements, personal recognitions, or a myriad of other accomplishments. To an extent, they are correct, but my parents taught my sister Anne and me that we should never fail to count our blessings and the harder we worked, the luckier we got. To a large extent, I believe that it is as accurate in this modern era as it was when I was growing up.

Unfortunately, many people in today's society believe that finances, grades, awards, and the like should be given and not earned. I call this the "Everybody Gets a Trophy" or "Participation Trophy" syndrome. They do not believe in the time-honored "gold, silver, and bronze" achievements any more. For them, participation is the key. These people are found in education, sports, politics, and other professions and I believe that they do immeasurable harm to the young and old whom they are counseling and influencing.

At an early age, parents should teach their children the value of having a good WORK ETHIC. Of all the other attributes, I firmly believe that this is one of the more important ones. This was taught to me by my parents, and it helped to shape my life. My mother and father were extremely hard-working individuals, and they taught with words around the dinner table and by example with their actions. In writings, speeches, and private conversations, many times I have discussed an example of a work ethic lesson taught to me by my father. I will repeat it here.

When I was nine years old, an advertisement in a magazine caught my eye. I believe the magazine was *Boy's Life,* but I cannot be sure. The advertisement proposed the purchase of fifty fancy 8×10 wall placards with Bible verses written on them. The idea was to purchase them from the company at one price and sell them door-to-door at a higher price. Again, I cannot be sure, but I believe that the purchase price for each one was $.50 and they were to be sold for $1.00. If all were sold, this would mean a $25.00 profit for the seller. Can you imagine what a $25.00 profit meant to a nine-year-old boy in 1950?

My Daddy approved this venture for me and agreed to provide the up-front money in the form of a loan. Before I could move forward, however, I was given a lesson on how to dress, the importance of looking the person in the eye, what to emphasize, knowledge of the verses, and in general how to approach the homeowner. After Daddy went over these instructions several times, he told me to go outside, ring the doorbell and make my sales pitch. I went outside and rang the doorbell. Daddy answered by saying, "Hello young man. What can I do for you?" I had one hand in my pocket and several sheets of paper representing the placards in the other hand. Daddy later told me that I was twisting and grinning and looking all around as I was beginning my sales pitch. He promptly shut the door in my face.

I didn't understand, therefore, I rang the doorbell again. He opened the door and repeated his greeting. I said, "Why did you shut the door in my face?" He said, "Because you did not act like you were serious about what you were selling."

He again went over the approach that I should use. He said that I should explain what I was selling and why I thought that it would be a good idea for the homeowners to buy. He further admonished me for grinning and moving around when I talked. The objective of Daddy's lesson centered on and emphasized knowledge of the subject, eye contact and appearance, benefits to the homeowner, physical demeanor, mental attitude, confidence in telling the story, articulations, and the all-important financial transaction. I was not to sell any of the placards on credit or accept partial payments. I strongly recommend that as many parents as possible teach this lesson that my father taught me.

After this second lesson, I went outside again, rang the doorbell, and proceeded with my sales talk. Daddy then said, "I think you are ready and I will loan you the money to purchase your first batch of placards."

I have never forgotten this lesson and continue to be appreciative for it. By the way, not only did I sell the first batch of fifty placards, but ended up selling a total of five orders of fifty placards each. I went to every home in the surrounding neighborhoods and practically everyone purchased one or two placards. Approximately twenty-five years later, I visited a lady who was in her late eighties and saw one of my Bible verses hanging on her wall. Seeing this caused me to swell up with emotion and pride.

Parents, just as I have never forgotten that lesson about work ethic, your sharing comparable work ethic lessons with your children will likely leave a lasting impression. The satisfaction of having a job and bringing in some money, no matter the amount, is indescribable. Young people should be taught that not only does legitimate employment earn money, but it builds confidence, self-esteem, and aids in the maturation process.

Individuals at all levels speak of the joy and importance of a job. In one of his last public speeches, on March 31, 1968, before he was assassinated, Dr. Martin Luther King, Jr. talked about the importance of work. It was his opinion that if a man didn't have a job, he would not be free to pursue happiness.[6]

Dr. King was correct. There is dignity in labor! Unfortunately, in some instances, individuals who do not get the salary that they would like or feel that the job is beneath them, do not work at all.

An example of this kind of thinking can be found in a decision by a son of one of my colleagues who turned down an opportunity to work at a fast-food establishment between his junior and senior years in college because he would have earned "only $225.00 before returning to college." This was a part-time, minimum wage job and, therefore, he had no interest. I believe that the parents should have counseled the young man to take the job for a number of reasons. The $225.00 could have assisted in buying his books, clothes, toiletries, or other essentials. Part of the $225.00 could have even allowed him to take his girlfriend on a date.

Let me acknowledge that teaching young people the value of work is more difficult today because so many of our youth have become slaves to an entitlement philosophy. Many do not understand the importance of having a good work ethic. They believe, or have been taught, that they are entitled to everything that others have received or are receiving, whether they have worked for it or not. In many instances, parents are the ones who have planted this negative seed. Parents should understand that in an attempt to show love and support, they are actually damaging future interactions that their child may have with other individuals.

Let me give an example of this negative entitlement thinking. During the latter half of May 2021, Hampton's Dean of Admission informed me of an email she had received from a prospective student complaining about not receiving a merit scholarship. The student stated that fourteen other institutions had offered him a merit scholarship and Hampton University had not. Upon analysis, the Dean found out that the student had a 2.6 grade point average. She informed the young man, "Please note that Hampton University is a first-rate institution with high standards. Students must have a cumulative 3.3 grade point average to be considered for merit awards and you presented a 2.6 cumulative weighted grade point average and a 2.5 unweighted GPA." Therefore, without casting aspersion on other institutions, Hampton University tries very hard to promote high standards on everything that is done.

It is important for individuals to know that whatever you work hard to achieve will have a greater impact on your life than that which may be given to you freely, requiring no effort of your own. When you don't work for what you have, oftentimes you will not appreciate it nor the person who provided it. In other words, you will not be truly grateful. Never forget that gratitude is a virtue.

SERVICE TO OTHERS

Helping others is truly one of the greatest gifts that an individual can bestow on another. The help, support, or service can be demonstrated in a number of different ways. One can donate time, money, clothes, care for a sick family member, friend, loved one, or a stranger. One can also volunteer as a leader or mentor with an organization like the Boy, Girl, or Brownie Scouts. Those that are athletic minded could serve as a coach to girls' and boys' softball, baseball, football, soccer, basketball, lacrosse, or other sports teams.

There are a plethora of nonprofit organizations that one can volunteer to serve with as well. Some of these include, but by no means are limited to the following: community action programs, food banks, Habitat for Humanity, The Salvation Army, Transitions Family Violence Services, youth commissions, United Way, medical support teams, rescue missions, Head Start, Agency on Aging, and

Catholic Charities. The important thing is to develop a mindset to be of service to others where possible.

Helping and being of service to others is something that my mother and father taught my sister Anne and me as early as I can remember. They said that it did not make any difference who it was, or how small or large the deed. The important thing was to be of service to others. It is no surprise then that my commitment to service dates back to my childhood.

Clearly there has been a frightening decline over the years in individuals' commitment to service. Dr. Martin Luther King, Jr. stated, "Everybody can be great . . . because anybody can serve. You don't have to have a college degree to serve. You don't have to make your subject and verb agree to serve. You only need a heart full of grace. A soul generated by love."[7]

Some may say that their financial, educational, and social status prevent them from being of service to others. This is not so. All that is needed is for parents, guardians, teachers, ministers, politicians, and others to emphasize that helping people is important and needed. Clearly, there has been a frightening decline over the years in individuals' commitment to service.

Over a number of decades, the United States has seen a relaxing of values, standards, and a coarsening of our culture. I first noticed this relaxing of standards when I observed junior and senior high school teachers being permitted to work in jeans and tennis shoes. It was about this time that media and other reports began to surface that there was a significant increase in physical and verbal attacks on teachers by students. The prevailing thought by many teacher training programs, teachers' unions, and educators at that time was that approaching students on their level by dressing, talking, and in many ways acting like them allowed the teachers to seem more caring and therefore the knowledge taught would be more readily acceptable. A recent example involved the president of a public university who was photographed dancing and drinking with students at a bar. His explanation and defense was that he wanted to be approachable and students had asked that he "speak to them in their language."

Although still practiced in many schools today, this theory about "approachability," "getting on their level," and "speaking in their lingo," has proven to be an abject failure. What has happened is that many students now see their teachers as their equals and have demonstrated a greater disrespect for them. As a result, there are more instances of verbal assaults, including cursing and physical abuse.

When I taught US History and civics in junior and senior high schools in the 1960s, all of the male teachers, at the very least, wore neckties every day. The female teachers wore dresses or skirts. Later, when the females began to wear pants to work, they wore dress pants—not jeans. During these times, appropriate teacher attire was discussed and emphasized by school administrators as a way to lead by example.

In my judgment, teachers and administrators at all levels who dressed, talked in the vocabulary of the street, socialized with students in an attempt to be "approachable" or "relate to them" began what has become generations of disservice to the learning process.

The educational establishment is not the only one that has aided and abetted this deterioration of our culture. A main villain is the advertising and marketing professions. Look at the commercials on TV today. They show the actors and actresses in less than a flattering manner. Some may wonder, how can these ads sell a particular product with the unflattering look that so many of them have? I suppose the answer is by showing it a multiplicity of times it gets seared into the brain that this is a desired product. Other villains can be found among Wall Street executives and other Fortune 500 companies. Instead of being role models in their appearance, you see CEOs in casual attire, including jeans, polo shirts, T-shirts, and tennis shoes. Some may say that the casual attire makes no difference as long as the shareholder value is positive. These actions on the part of well-meaning people are equally as egregious as those educators who advocate "dumbing down" the curriculum to accommodate a certain racial or income level student.

Many successful people come from very humble beginnings. Let me use my hometown as an example. I come from a small town in Alabama where there was income inequality among the races and racism was officially sanctioned. However, people like my father and others taught those of us in the Black community that all people had potential, no matter the race or background. We were taught to set our goals high and to work hard to achieve those goals. As a result, this small town—Brewton, Alabama—produced African Americans who became extremely successful businessmen and women, heads of K-12 school systems—including the superintendent of schools in Chicago, Illinois, and the presidents of educational institutions such as Hampton University and Alabama State University. No one told us that because we were African Americans we could not achieve. No one said that because we came from families whose incomes may have been low, that our vision, expectations, and prospect for success had to be low. Quite the contrary, as we were told that we could achieve at the highest levels if we worked hard.

Unfortunately, there are many in our society today, including some politicians and those in the media who focus on race and income inequality and suggest those are reasons for not achieving. Actually, it is nothing but an excuse. I disavow this notion because my experience tells me that everyone has the potential and if given the opportunity can be successful.

We can get a strong work ethic and high standards back and parents can lead the way. Consider, if you will, that even the most disadvantaged members of our society are members who have something—if only their personal time—that might be used in service to another. All of us must have a collective commitment to service, and this requirement is more imperative today than it has ever been before.

This commitment can be on an individual basis. It can be a team effort. It can be in a neighborhood or city. It can also be a regional, state, national, or international level. Let me give you two examples.

The first is a team example and involves a situation where Hampton University provided a helping hand to students and their families from the University of the Bahamas who were displaced by Hurricane Dorian. This saga started with a phone call that I placed to Dr. Rodney Smith, the president of the University of the Bahamas. Dr. Smith was a former Administrative Vice President and Director of Planning at Hampton University. As a colleague and friend, I called him one evening just to check to see how he and his family were doing as a result of Hurricane Dorian. He told me that they were doing fine; however, the North Campus of the University of the Bahamas was almost completely obliterated. After we hung up, I thought about our conversation quite a bit. The next morning, immediately after getting out of bed, I called him and indicated that Hampton University would accept students for one semester from his North Campus so that their education would not be interrupted.

He obviously was very pleased and gave me the go-ahead to start planning. After notifying my Board of Trustees, I appointed an Action Task Force to provide a seamless transition for the students from the University of the Bahamas to continue their academic studies at Hampton. I appointed Dr. Pamela Moolenaar-Wirsiy to serve as Chair of this Task Force. Other Task Force members included Drs. JoAnn Haysbert, Kim Luckes, Kristie Norwood, Charrita Quimby, and Karen Williams; Dean Angela Boyd, Ms. Brint Martin, Ms. Denise Nichols, and Ms. Laura Tanganelli. The Task Force went to work immediately and met every afternoon with Dr. Wirsiy providing outstanding leadership. Interestingly enough, Dr. Wirsiy is a native of St. Thomas, U.S. Virgin Islands and graduated from Hampton with a Bachelor's in Biology. She was at Hampton University and at the time serving as an American Council in Education Fellow for the academic year 2019–20.

I indicated to the Task Force that Hampton University would provide free room, board, tuition, and fees to these students for one semester. Additionally, we would provide them with a cash stipend that would be helpful in the purchase of their books, toiletries, other incidentals, and assist with travel.

Within the first day, we received thirty-two positive responses and by the end of the third day, we had received 191. Hampton's Office of Admission, under the leadership of Dean Angela Boyd, began working immediately to get the Bahamian students I-20s processed so that they could secure visas to come into the United States. At my request, Dr. Smith selected a faculty member, Dr. Pandora Johnson from the University of the Bahamas, to serve as a liaison with Dr. Wirsiy. Both of these ladies provided outstanding leadership, coordination, and skill to make this initiative a reality. Dr. Johnson worked with students and parents to identify a central location where the students could pick up their I-20s; coordinated their travel from the University of the Bahamas North Campus in Freeport to Nassau;

worked with the Bahamian Embassy; and even though she had to leave on a business trip to the United Kingdom, stayed in touch with Dr. Wirsiy via talk, text, and email.

Dr. Wirsiy and the Action Task Force were simply outstanding! They elicited the support of student leaders, faculty, and administrators to ensure that the University of the Bahamas' students transition was well supported; made sure that the students had visas and health insurance; liaised with the faculty to enroll students in classes that aligned with their course of study at the University of the Bahamas; and coordinated the securing of clothing, toiletries, and supplies. Throughout all of this, we continue to receive very positive responses and media attention to our benevolence. Not only did we receive calls, letters, and emails, but we also received financial donations and other forms of support. As example, New Birth Baptist Church in Atlanta, Georgia, under the leadership of Pastor Jamal Bryant, and Jet Blue Airlines committed to paying for the airfare of all the students to travel to Hampton.

We also received large gifts from our Trustees including $100,000 from Zachary Scott; $25,000 from Trustee Calvin Butts; $10,000 from our alumnus Margot Copeland; and $5,000 from a former Trustee, Rodgin Cohen. In addition, we received gifts of $1,000, $800, $500, $300, $250, $200, $150, and twenty-six gifts of $100. There are were also twenty-five gifts ranging between $18.68 and $50. Some of these gifts were from alumni and friends of Hampton, while many were from individuals with no prior knowledge of Hampton who heard of our benevolence and wanted to contribute. As a result of these wonderful gifts, we increased the amount of cash that we provided the Bahamian students to $1,000.

Ultimately, there were forty-three students who came from the Bahamas and it was indeed a very smooth transition. Upon arrival, the students were transported to campus by a bus from Richmond, Virginia, and welcomed with open arms. They participated in an orientation which culminated in a welcome pep rally in the Student Center Atrium. Course schedules for these students that corresponded with their schedules at the University of the Bahamas were prepared. Their health insurance coverage was secured and Hampton provided them with required immunizations in partnership with a local pharmacy.

I will say to parents and others that this is service to humankind at its very best! Another aspect to this heartwarming story is the graciousness that the Bahamian students accepted Hampton's largess. There were, "thank yous," and tears of joy galore. Clearly, true gratitude is a virtue!

Though the previous example reflects the commitment to service as a team effort, let me give you an individual example of service to others. This is best represented in a proposal that I have been touting for approximately twenty years. That solution is the establishment of a mandate for a fourteen- or twenty-four-months mandatory national service for all citizens of the United States. I will use a personal example to illustrate.

After I finished college, I spent a total of three years in the United States Army in the service of this country. The rigor and discipline I was exposed to and that was required of me, without a doubt, helped me to become a man.

I can personally testify to the fact that it also helped a number of other persons. For example, in basic training I was a squad leader. In my squad I had two young people whose names were Charles P. Jones and Jerry Jones. They were Black and happened to be from the inner-city of Chicago. Two other young people in my squad, John E. Isenberg and Carrol D. Jones, happened to be from the mountains of Tennessee. They were White.

My recollection is that neither the Tennessee boys nor the Chicago boys had ever had an interaction with members of the opposite race. As a result of being in the army, in the same squad they learned something about different cultures, different attitudes, different thought processes, and the importance of teamwork in order to get things accomplished.

In my squad were other African American, Caucasian, and Native American men. Men from low-, middle-, and high-income backgrounds and men from divergent geographical locations. Yet during our service to our country, each of us reaped multiple personal benefits—benefits that proved to broaden our exposure to other people and cultures; enhanced our sensitivities; sharpened our intellect; shaped our character; developed our leadership abilities; and—most importantly—have remained a part of our makeup for the balance of our lives.

For those who do not want to exercise their national service obligation by being a part of the military, another option could be the establishment of a National Service Corps. After receiving the appropriate training, I can envision thousands of young men and women working all over this country in boys and girls clubs, recreational centers, battered women's shelters, wildlife parks, elementary school systems, and many other venues.

Suppose they wanted to go to college first. That could be accomplished because every teacher, businessman or woman, TV personality, newspaper reporter, social worker, scientist, artist, "doctor, lawyer or Indian Chief" might be assigned to an underserved area of the country in order to fulfill their national service obligation.

Think about it. A teacher, social worker, or doctor who had not completed his national service obligation could do so by serving others in some organized capacity. Still another option could be Foreign Service in the Peace Corps.

So, you see, the options could be many. It could be in the National Service Corps. It could be the military. It could be in the mountains of Tennessee. It could be in the inner-city of Chicago, or it could be tutoring kindergarten students in Baltimore, Maryland, or in Painted Post, New York.

The length of service that I propose is either fourteen or twenty-four months. This would include two months of discipline, rigor, and training and twelve or twenty-two months of actual service.

Just one or two years. In that amount of time and through continual rotation, nearly every ill that plagues our society might well be eradicated or at least greatly diminished. While serving, those providing the service would likely reap all the inherent benefits associated with giving of themselves and benefit personally from the training and interaction with others. My proposal is not at all complicated, but it does require the sincere interest and efforts of us all.

The initiation of a national service option could realistically result in a win-win situation. An imperative component of this proposal is that it must have a fair and equal application for every American, notwithstanding income levels, geographical location, educational backgrounds, financial status, or political clout of the family. It will not work unless it is equal and fair across the board. Every American unless mentally impaired, would be eligible to complete either fourteen or twenty-four months of national service.

If that were to happen, I firmly believe that our young people would not only provide a service, but they also would become better citizens and, subsequently, adults. You would see more humanity and less hate. You would see more civility and less cynicism. You would see more discipline and less destruction. You would see more compassion and less conflict. You would see more responsibility and less rage. You would see more patience and less intolerance. You would see more ownership in society and less of the feeling that society owes something to someone. In short, you would see more of a desire to make this great nation of ours a better place in which to live.

Until such initiatives are once again woven into the fabric of American culture, there are immediate ways in which we might commit our service to others. Individuals could give of their resources. They could find the time to serve on boards. They could tutor and/or lecture in a variety of settings. They could make time to serve as a big brother or big sister.

For me, service is truly an exhilarating experience. To realize how one's own efforts might influence the less fortunate is exciting, inspirational, and gratifying. Lack of this realization may well be the obstacle that prohibits our commitment to service.

Parents can be a major influence in reviving this wavering commitment to service and enliven our responsibility to one another. Somehow, we must convince young people, politicians, media types, educators, and others to do everything possible to bring back the culture of kindness and civility to our society. Service to others is a vehicle to achieving that goal.

The Hampton University alma mater contains the lyrics, "O Hampton, we never can make thee a song, except as our lives do the singing. In service that will thy great spirit prolong and send it through centuries ringing!" If those in the world at large would allow their lives to do the singing through service, I am convinced that the song of life would be the sweetest refrain imaginable.

CHAPTER IV

FINANCING
HIGHER EDUCATION TODAY

Providing access to and opportunities in higher education have never been more dependent on finances than they are today. Parents and students should not allow finances to discourage them, however, because there are options that can be explored, including personal savings plans, individual state 529 plans, corporate scholarships, federal student aid programs, corporate relief plans, and others. Let's examine these options.

PERSONAL SAVINGS PLANS

Family contributions resulting from savings plans not only provide financial flexibility for a number of different kinds of future needs and opportunities, but also teach a valuable lesson. That lesson is that it is not wise to spend 100 percent of one's income, no matter the source of that income. Too many people of all ages overspend on items they want, rather than purchasing essential items first. In that regard, some parents seem to have a difficult time accepting their role in financing a child's education. Recognizing that financial support rests first with the family cannot be emphasized enough. Every family should consider developing a successful financial plan that includes the use of personal financial resources. The first step in developing such a plan begins with the establishment of a savings mentality.

Developing the discipline to consistently save has proven difficult for some. Therefore, parents should start by considering their children's needs rather than their wants. In a time and era where so much emphasis is placed on brands and not brains, parents would do well to understand that their son does not need to purchase the $150–$200 top brand sneakers rather than perfectly acceptable less expensive brands. How about the costs of a daughter's trips to the nail and hair salons? Does your child really need to have her nails professionally manicured every other week? In many instances, a trip to the nail salon is equal to the cost of an application fee at a college or university. Electronic devices such as smartphones, tablets, and computers are considered essential items in today's society, but to have the top-of-the-line product or latest version of these devices every time a new one comes out is not a requirement for a fifteen-year-old! Designer handbags and trendy clothes are nice, but developing healthy spending habits is nicer.

Wise spending should be a priority as well as a practice. There are also those mothers and fathers who in trying to "keep up with the Joneses," either purchase or encourage their children to purchase the expensive, trendy things that they do not really need. Do teenagers and young adults really need expensive, personal accoutrements, such as a $175–$200 pair of jeans, $600–$800 shoes, $1,000 boots, and $300 cologne? Unfortunately, too many people pay for what they want and beg for what they need. If money is available, there is no problem in acquiring these high-priced items, but everyone should take care of their responsibilities first. Discipline and diligence are important characteristics necessary for building financial stability.

Families that prioritize desires over needs do not exemplify wise parenting. Therefore, I advise individuals, no matter their income, to get into the habit of saving for future priorities, especially for their child's education. Although there are different ways to save, I am not one who believes in stashing money in cookie jars, between mattresses, or some other place around the house. My experience has been to establish a savings account at a financial institution and develop the discipline to save something from each check no matter the source of the funds.

From the time that I was nine years old through my teen-age years, I had menial jobs such as picking cotton, mowing lawns, hoeing and shaking peanuts, and going door-to-door selling Bible placards to be hung on walls. With the money that I earned from these jobs, my parents encouraged me to open a savings account at a local bank and put something in the account every week. This I did, although it was only $2.00 each week. The joy and satisfaction that I received by getting on my bike every Saturday morning and riding to the bank, walking inside and up to the teller's cage, and giving her a small portion of my hard-earned money was indescribable. I can say that the feeling of courage, confidence, and equality as an African American, walking into a White financial institution in the state of Alabama in the 1950s and being welcomed with smiles and respect is still with me today.

When I graduated from high school in 1957, my savings account had ballooned to approximately $500. The $500 made me think that I was rich! My parents were obviously as pleased as I was, but suggested that I use $100 of that amount as book money the next year while away in college. Not only did I take their advice, but I remember being extremely pleased that I was helping my parents with my college bills. The philosophy of saving something from every paycheck, that my parents taught me as a young boy, was ingrained in me and I have continued that practice to the present day. It has served me and my family well.

It is important for all individuals to have a personal savings plan. Such a plan provides financial flexibility for a number of different kinds of future needs and opportunities. The financial advice I give to seniors graduating from college is to "pay yourself first." I encourage them to save something from every check because I want them to develop a savings mentality and establish a pattern of saving early in their professional careers. Many young people today feel that they do not have enough money to save because they have the financial burden of student loans.

If you are or should you become one of the many Americans facing student loan debt, I encourage you to take advantage of the ways for borrowers to reduce student debt mentioned later. Even if you are not eligible for any of the plans, you should not allow your student loan payments to deter you from having a personal savings plan.

Wise spending should be a priority as well as a practice. Once you have saved money, it is important to spend the remaining income in a responsible manner. The first step in spending wisely involves determining the difference between needs and wants. Needs are the basic essentials in life that are necessary for survival, such as food, shelter, and clothing. All of these items can be purchased at different price points, so it is important to make these purchases based on your income and your ability to pay for them without accumulating debt.

Allow me to explain what I mean about the difference between needs and wants as it relates to basic essentials. Buying groceries to have food on the table is a need, but eating out at expensive restaurants multiple times during a week is a want. Having clean water to drink is a need. Although they may appear to be needs, cigarettes, beer, wine, and alcohol are definitely wants!

It is not necessary to rent or purchase housing that requires you to use the majority of your income to make payments. For a family of four, 1,500 sq. ft. of space may be considered a need, but 4,000 sq. ft. of space is definitely a want. I don't recommend spending $200 or more on brand name sneakers, jeans, handbags, and other expensive items when you cannot afford to do so. Clothing is a basic need, but expensive jeans and handbags are wants, for sure!

The second step in spending wisely is taking care of financial responsibilities first. It is not wise to spend money on non-essential items before taking care of essential expenses for housing, utilities, food, transportation, and making payments on student loans and credit cards.

Let me stop here and encourage you to keep your credit card debt at an absolute minimum. The amount of money you spend paying the interest on these purchases is money that you could have saved or used to pay cash for those same items. In my opinion, you should pay for credit card purchases as soon as possible. It is not wise to allow charges to sit so that interest compounds to the point where it takes years to reduce or pay off the balance.

It is my belief that individuals at any income level can have a savings mentality and spend wisely when they determine the difference between needs and wants as well as be responsible in their spending. If this is done properly, you can take care of your essential needs as well as enjoy some of your wants. You just cannot go overboard! Establishing a budget can be helpful in preventing overspending.

Developing a savings mentality and spending wisely require discipline. In order to save, you may have to forego some of your wants. This may seem difficult, but I assure you that it will be beneficial in the long run. The money that you save will be available to you long-term whereas many of the non-essential items you sacrifice to save money would only have lasted a short period of time.

Will this philosophy of saving work for everyone? I believe so! It is a reality that there are low-, middle-, and high-income families in this country. No matter the income, my thinking is that everyone could and should save something from every paycheck. There may be those with a low income who disagree with the philosophy; however, some of these same individuals buy cigarettes, beer, wine, and other non-essential items when they receive their checks. I believe that people at all income levels can do both. They can save and also enjoy some of their desires.

Let's look at some concrete examples. As we review these numbers, remember that there is a difference between gross and net income. Gross pay is the total amount of the income earned before taxes are taken out. Net pay is what is actually received. This is sometimes referred to as take-home pay. Suppose a family is on welfare. Does that stop them from saving? Depending on the particular state, welfare agencies provide a cash allowance for four or five months in addition to income for childcare, food, medical, and utility assistance. The national average cash disbursement for a qualified low-income family of four in this country is approximately $900 per month tax-free. This allowance is called Temporary Assistance for Needy Families (TANF). The most generous state allowance is Alaska, which provides $923 a month for a family of three, with Alabama providing approximately $170 a month, which is the lowest.

Recipients of TANF may also work as long as the total monthly income does not exceed their particular state's maximum.

No matter the source (part-time, full-time, TANF), suppose the take-home pay is $1,000 per month, which equals $12,000 per year. If this person or family saved 5 percent, or $50 per month, in eighteen years the minimum saved would be $10,800. A gross income of $2,000 per month would total $24,000 per year or a net pay of approximately $19,542 per year. Five percent of $19,542 equals $977 per year or $81.45 per month. After eighteen years, the $81.45 would produce a minimum of $17,593. Any interest gained, no matter how small, would offset taxes paid and could increase the $17,593 significantly. Whatever the amount, after eighteen years, coupled with other federal, state, and private aid, the savings could be the difference between a child attending an institution of higher education or going to work immediately at a lower paying job.

On the other hand, a family bringing home a higher wage could afford to put aside a higher amount for their children's education. A person making $4,000 per month has a total salary of $48,000 per year. Five percent of $4,000 per month is $200 or $50 per week. In eighteen years, the $50 per week would total $43,200. Six thousand dollars a month equals $72,000, and $8,000 totals $96,000 per year. Taking into consideration that taxes must be paid and necessities taken care of, it is clear that a family making approximately $50,000, $75,000, or $100,000 per year could save at least 5 percent of their monthly take-home pay for their child's education and still pursue the lifestyle and comfort that middle-class families enjoy.

Think of the positive impact that just a little discipline would produce for a child or children in these families. It boggles the mind what discipline and foresight would do for families making considerably more than the examples above.

Clearly, there are parents who put material things, travel, and social expenses before educational expenses for their children. Just as clearly, there are parents who put the health, welfare, and education of their children first. It would be great if there were more people who understood that even when they put the health, welfare, and education of their children first, there may still be opportunity to purchase material items, travel, and socialize.

Another problem, as stated earlier, that some of our young people face today is associated with parents who do not understand that it is their responsibility before anyone or anything else to educate their children. Too many in our culture today want others to do what parents have historically done and should continue to do. We hear that supposedly responsible people talk about free tuition, free healthcare, free universal childcare, total loan forgiveness, and other giveaways. They want the federal or state governments, institutions, wealthy individuals, or some other entity to do what they should be doing. This kind of "pie in the sky" thinking does immeasurable harm to our children and our society. In discussing the inalienable rights of life, liberty, and the pursuit of happiness, Dr. Martin Luther King, Jr. said that, "If a man doesn't have a job or an income, he has neither life, nor liberty, nor the possibility for the pursuit of happiness. He merely exists."[1] This is the kind of philosophy that all of us should be teaching and striving to achieve. Educating our children and instilling in them a good work ethic will help all of us reach our goals. Having a job to earn money is important, but knowing how to manage the money we earn is just as important. Without a doubt, my recommendation is to initiate a savings account at a financial institution and save a minimum amount early and often.

Managing personal finances is a major part of life, and it has a great impact on every aspect of our lives. There are people who manage their money well and those who manage it poorly. Often, the way people manage money is determined by how they saw money being managed within their households when they were young. Most follow these same patterns, good or bad. Others choose an entirely different pattern based on acquired knowledge from teachers, mentors, or their own reading in books such as this one.

COLLEGE SAVINGS PLANS (529)

In addition to personal savings accounts, another excellent savings tool can be found in 529 plans, so named for Section 529 of the Internal Revenue Code. The 529 provision of the IRS Code is comprised of two components—college savings and prepaid tuition. The prepaid tuition plan is not available nationwide, but the college savings component is available in all fifty states and the District of Columbia. Eligible institutions include colleges, universities, trade and vocational schools, community colleges, theological seminaries, internationals schools, and study abroad programs run through U.S. eligible schools.[2]

The 529 programs are attractive because they serve the dual purpose of saving for college and providing a tax advantage. An individual's contributions are not tax deductible, but any growth and earnings are tax exempt.[3] The plans are so flexible that practically anyone can participate.

The college component sponsored by the state of Wisconsin called "Tomorrow's Scholar" allows one to participate for as little as $25 per month. Although sponsored in Wisconsin, this plan is sold nationwide.[4] Others, like "College America," which is sponsored by the Commonwealth of Virginia, permit an account to be opened for just $250.[5]

There is no question that 529 programs help a large number of families prepare for college. In addition to coaxing and assisting in the development of a savings mentality, 529 plans are also helpful in some of the following ways.

1. They alert individuals and families that they are responsible and need to plan for their children's education.
2. Contributions from grandparents for tuition may be excluded from annual gift-tax allowance.
3. They establish the importance of a savings mentality.
4. They remind families that discipline is important and needed to achieve goals and objectives.
5. They provide lessons in financial investing.
6. They permit growth in investments without paying taxes on the appreciation.
7. Ultimately, they provide the opportunity for children and family members to experience, learn, and gain proficiency in a chosen field.
8. They do not count as assets on the FAFSA.

The 529 Prepaid Tuition Plan is not available in all states and institutions as of yet. The plan, where available, allows students and families to pay for future tuition costs at their preferred institution's current tuition rate at the time that the money for the plan is provided. For those families who can afford it, this particular plan can save a great deal of money. Think about it, tuition costs at any post-secondary institution today will be considerably less expensive than they will be in sixteen or eighteen years from now.

CORPORATE SCHOLARSHIPS

A large number of corporations of various sizes, assets, products, and purposes are sponsoring scholarships for high school graduates along with traditional ones for their employees. Just as there are differences in the corporations, the stated reasons for providing the scholarships and the amounts of scholarship dollars are also different. Perhaps the major motivating factor is the need to train and retrain new and existing employees. Therefore, an investment in talent is good business.

Criteria for these scholarships also vary with the corporations. Some base awards on need, merit, or disability; community service; demonstrated leadership; under-represented women and minorities; academic interests; or study in a specific area. Whatever the motivation, the participating corporations are providing a valuable service. A look at a few of the corporate offerings illustrate this diversity in amounts and purposes of the scholarships.

GOOGLE provides scholarships and programs for a wide variety of recipients. Some examples include their Generations Scholarship, Student Veterans of America Scholarship, Women Techmakers Scholars, Computer Science Summer Institute, Lime Scholarship, and the AISES Scholarship. These and other Google Scholarships support students who are minorities, including American Indians, women, veterans, summer institute participants, and others who aspire to excel in computer technology. One or more of these programs are open to students in the United States, Canada, Europe, the Middle East, Africa, and the Asia Pacific. Recipients receive up to $10,000 in the United States and $5,000 in Canada, depending on the need and the specific program. Google's goals are ". . . to provide scholarships and programs to encourage students to excel in their studies and become active role models and leaders." They do an excellent job in their stated objectives.[6]

COCA-COLA Scholars program has provided over $69 million to students who are graduating from high school. This soft drink company awards fifty scholarships each on an annual basis of $1,500, $1,250, and $1,000 for two-year colleges. This program is called the Community College Academic Team and is administered by Phi Theta Kappa. They also provide 200 scholarships of $1,000 each to students at community colleges under the heading of Leaders of Promise. This too is designed for students enrolled in a community college. Coca-Cola's big splash, however, is its Scholars Program Scholarship. This program awards 150 scholarships of $20,000 each on an annual basis. This is outstanding! These scholarships are based on achievements and are awarded to seniors who are graduating from high school.[7]

BURGER KING Scholarships are administered by the James W. McLamore Scholarship program which is a programmatic component of the Burger King James W. McLamore Foundation. The foundation's mission is ". . . to create brighter futures by empowering individuals and feeding potential through education and emergency relief."[8] Awards range from $1,000 to $50,000 with $5,000 for regional winners. The recipients are high school students, along with Burger King employees and their families. Winners are selected after an evaluation of their grade point averages, work experiences, and extracurricular activities, including community service.

The DELL SCHOLARS program offers a holistic approach to support for college-bound students. Confidential counseling, financial aid coaching, and support staff mentoring in addition to a monetary award is provided to help the Dell scholars succeed. The financial help comes in the form of $20,000, a laptop, and textbook credits. Some of the requirements as a Dell Scholar include completion of a Dell approved College Readiness Program in the eleventh and twelfth grades; meeting the requirements for a federal Pell grant, which means that there must be a demonstrated financial need; enrollment in an accredited post-secondary institution the next fall following the senior year of high school; and earning at least a 2.4 grade point average. Dell's unique approach ". . . targets low-income, highly motivated students who are better than their numbers indicate and demonstrate the drive to succeed despite personal obstacles."[9]

TYLENOL FUTURE CARE SCHOLARSHIPS are awarded to students who are interested in the health-care field. Specifically, a student must be a senior in college or graduate school and a resident of one of the fifty states, Puerto Rico, or the District of Columbia. Programs of study include medicine, nursing, dentistry, pharmacy, physical therapy, or other health-care fields. To further their objective of providing support for students who want to be health-care providers, Tylenol, which is a subsidiary of the medical devices, pharmaceutical, and consumer packed goods manufacturing company, Johnson & Johnson, allocates ten $10,000 and thirty $5,000 non-renewable grants per year.[10]

One of MICROSOFT's scholarship programs is designed for students enrolled in a full-time bachelor's degree program at a four-year college or university. Eligible students must have a demonstrated record of academic achievement and maintain a 3.0 cumulative GPA in an undergraduate degree program in computer science, computer engineering, electrical engineering, or a related STEM field. The scholarship funds cover a portion or all tuition costs and paid registration, travel, hotel, and meals to a diversity conference dealing with women in computing, Black, or Hispanic engineers. Recipients must utilize the tuition grant funds for full-time study at a four-year, post-secondary institution located in the United States, Canada, or Mexico. The number and amounts of scholarships awarded vary each year, with the total amount being approximately $500,000. Applicants must submit a transcript, complete an essay, and demonstrate leadership, financial need, and academic achievement. Microsoft is on record as advocating college scholarship support for African Americans, Hispanics, women, and those with disabilities.

For example, they have a specifically designed program entitled Blacks at Microsoft Scholarships. This program is designed for high school seniors and administered by the Blacks at Microsoft organization. Interested students and parents can get more information on student financial support on all of their programs by contacting the Microsoft Scholarship Program at the Microsoft Corporation in Redmond, Washington.[11]

Practically every major corporation in this country has a scholarship program designed to increase and/or improve their own subject specific area of business for those individuals who have been historically under-represented in the workforce. The corporations listed above are merely examples to illustrate the point that funding is available to support college students from a variety of business sources. They differ in amounts, lengths, purpose, and citizenship requirements for eligible recipients, but diligence on the part of parents and students may result in needed financial support for a college education.

FEDERAL STUDENT AID PROGRAMS

There is a myriad of federal programs designed to be of assistance to college students matriculating at institutions of higher education. These include grants such as Pell Grant; Federal Supplemental Educational Opportunity Grant (FSEOG); Teacher Education Assistance for College and Higher Education (TEACH Grant); and Iraq and Afghanistan Service Grant. Other aid includes federal work study and loans such as Direct Subsidized Loan; Direct Unsubsidized Loan; and Direct PLUS Loan. The following listing outlines the types of aid, eligibility, and program information taken directly from the U.S. Department of Education Federal Student Aid Brochure.

Types of Federal Student Aid: Grants, Work-Study, and Loans[12]

GRANTS	
Programs and Type of Aid	**Eligibility and Program Information**
Federal Pell Grant Grant: does not have to be repaid	For undergraduates with financial need who have not earned bachelor's or professional degrees; in some cases, a student enrolled in a postbaccalaureate teacher certification program may also receive a Federal Pell Grant. A student can receive a Federal Pell Grant for no more than 12 semesters or the equivalent (roughly six years).
Federal Supplemental Education Opportunity Grant (FSEOG) Grant: does not have to be repaid	For undergraduates with exceptional financial need; Federal Pell Grant recipients take priority; funds depend on availability at school.
Teacher Education Assistance for College and Higher Education (TEACH) Grant Grant: does not have to be repaid unless converted to a Direct Unsubsidized Loan for failure to carry out teaching service obligation as promised.	For undergraduate, postbaccalaureate, and graduate students who are completing or plan to complete course work needed to begin a career in teaching. As a condition for receiving this grant, a student must sign a *TEACH Grant Agreement to Serve* in which the student agrees to perform four years of qualifying teaching service and meet other requirements.

Programs and Type of Aid	Eligibility and Program Information
Iraq and Afghanistan Service Grant Grant: does not have to be repaid	For students who are not Pell-eligible only because they have less financial need than is required to receive Pell funds. A student's parent or guardian must have died as a result of military service in Iraq or Afghanistan after the events of 9/11. A student can receive an Iraq and Afghanistan Service Grant for no more than 12 semesters or the equivalent (roughly six years).
WORK-STUDY	
Federal Work-Study Work-Study: money is earned; does not have to be repaid	For undergraduate and graduate students; part-time jobs can be on campus or off campus. Money is earned while attending school.
LOANS	
Direct Subsidized Loan Loan: must be repaid with interest	For undergraduate students who have financial need; the U.S. Department of Education generally pays interest while the student is in school and during certain other periods; a student must be enrolled at least half-time. The interest rate is 4.45% for loans first disbursed on or after July 1, 2019, and before July 1, 2020, and fixed for the life of the loan. Borrowers may not receive this type of loan for more than 150 percent of the length of their program of study; the U.S. Department of Education may stop paying interest if a student who received Direct Subsidized Loans for the maximum period continues enrollment.

Programs and Type of Aid	Eligibility and Program Information
Direct Unsubsidized Loan Loan: must be repaid with interest	For undergraduate and graduate or professional students; the borrower is responsible for interest during all periods; a student must be enrolled at least half-time; financial need is not required. The interest rate is 4.45% (undergraduate) and 6% (graduate or professional) for loans first distributed on or after July 1, 2019, and before July 1, 2020, and fixed for the life of the loan.
Direct PLUS Loan Loan: must be repaid with interest	For parents of dependent or undergraduate students and for graduate or professional students; the borrower is responsible for interest during all periods; a student must be enrolled at least half-time; financial need is not required; the borrower must not have adverse credit history. The interest rate is 7% for loans first distributed on or after July 1, 2019, and before July 1, 2020, and fixed for the life of the loan.

Of all the programs listed above, the ones dealing with the student loans have proven to be the most popular forms of financing post-secondary education today. They are also the most problematic and are receiving the most attention now due to the sizable amount that is owed to the federal government. As of 2021 that amount was $1.6 trillion, which is over a 150 percent increase in just the last decade.[13] How did we get to this point when this debt is not only a burden on students and their families, but on the national economy as well?

Although Harvard initiated aid to needy students as early as 1840, it was not until the mid-1900s that American higher education institutions began looking at a uniform formula for determining students' financial needs. John Monro, a man that I knew and greatly respected when he worked at Miles College in Alabama, originated a need-based formula to assist in awarding needy students financial aid for study at Harvard. This was the early 1950s and Monro was the Director of Financial Aid at Harvard University. Monro's formula included a very simple 15 percent rule to determine a student's eligibility. A student's family was expected to contribute 15 percent of the cost and Harvard would award the difference.[14]

In 1953, Monro presented his idea of everybody using the same criteria for determining need analysis at a College Board symposium. This led to the creation of the College Scholarship Service (CSS) in 1954 with approximately one hundred institutions utilizing this formula.[15]

It was not until the 1950s that the first federal loan program came into existence. Specifically, the 1958 National Defense Student Loan Program (NDSL) later renamed the Perkins Loan Program was initiated. These loans went to the colleges and universities for distribution rather than directly to the students.

During the 1960s, the United States went through a metamorphosis in a number of areas, including race relations, culture, and education. It was a time of change, protests, and reform. In race relations, the 1964 Civil Rights Act, first proposed by President John F. Kennedy and signed into law by President Lyndon B. Johnson passed. This Act prohibited discrimination in employment by race, religion, sex, and national origin. It also prohibited segregation in public places.

Culturally, students and others demanded an end to the Vietnam War, challenged political norms, and were advocates for gender equity. More and more people began to embrace the concept of leveling the playing field by giving women and minorities more access and opportunity. This concept, desire, and demand did not escape the politicians of both parties. As it relates to students in higher education, President Lyndon Johnson wanted to establish a need-based scholarship program, but the U.S. Congress, under pressure from their constituents, wanted to include provisions for middle-class students. In the end, they compromised and did both with the creation of the Guaranteed Student Loan (GSL) program, later called Stafford Loans.

In 1964, Federal Work Study (FWS) was created. The program allowed students to work part-time either on or off campus. The motivation for the FWS was to assist students from low income backgrounds with their college expenses.[16]

The prevailing mood of the country in the 1960s clearly began to tilt increasingly toward a society that valued social justice and reform. This included more and better access for women, minorities, and others who had been discriminated against in the past. As it related to the educational establishment, the U.S. Congress wanted to do more to support student goals in education.

This led to the Higher Education Act (HEA) of 1965. The HEA initiated the Educational Opportunity Grant (EOG) program designed for undergraduates with a demonstrated need. In an effort to consolidate the federal student aid programs, the Perkins Loan and College Work Study programs were transferred to those designated to administer the Higher Education Act.

In the 1970s, Congress expanded the federal loan programs even more. It almost seemed as if the desire to provide more and more loans without collateral became contagious. Four new federally guaranteed loan programs became law. These included the Subsidized Stafford Loans, Unsubsidized Stafford Loans, Parent PLUS Loans, and Federal Consolidation Loans. As a part of the 1972 Higher Education Act reauthorization, the Student Loan Marketing Association (Sallie Mae) was initiated to increase liquidity for the Stafford Loan Program. Designed to provide assistance to students in need, the Basic Educational Opportunity Grant (BEOG) was also initiated.[17]

These Congressional approvals clearly helped an exceedingly large number of students to attend institutions of higher education. As positive as the increased students' college matriculation may be, over the years, the members of Congress, as well as the various Administrations, did not put into place strong management policies, procedures, and safeguards for a realistic repayment of the borrowed funds. As a result, loan debt increased significantly.

By 1986, student and parent debt had ballooned to almost $10 billion.[18] During this time, many of my fellow college presidents and I saw the crisis that this easy money was creating and warned against it. We were in favor of loans, but we wanted more fiscal responsibility and accountability built into the programs. Unfortunately, no one listened to us, and if they did, they did not put the management and fiscal safeguards in place.

Perhaps no one heeded our concern because so many of the opinion makers, including administrative officials, members of Congress, policy advocates, economists, education officials, and others were convinced that the stated goals of more access to college for everyone; empowerment of women, minorities, and low-income families; and increased earnings were worthy at any cost. Indeed they were worthy; however, fiscal responsibility through government oversight should have been initiated from the beginning.

Throughout the 1990s and into the 2000s, the number and amount of loans continued to grow. In 1992, for example, as a part of the reauthorization of the Higher Education Act, the loan limits, as well as the number of loans, were increased substantially. Annual loan limits for dependent students were increased from $4,000 to $5,500 for use in their third and fourth years, with an aggregate limit increase from $17,250 to $23,000. The 1992 reauthorization also saw the creation of the Unsubsidized Stafford Loan Program. This program was designed to include students from middle-class families although, unlike the subsidized loans, there were no interest subsidies while they were still matriculating.[19]

Today, the loan limits are considerably higher and subject to change. For dependent students the maximum for the first year is $5,500 with up to $3,500 in subsidized loans; $6,500 with up to $4,500 in subsidized loans for the second year; and $7,500 with up to $5,500 in subsidized loans for the third year and beyond. The total loan that a student may receive is $31,000 with up to $23,000 in subsidized loans. Independent students are eligible for a great deal more than dependent ones. Undergraduates may receive up to $57,500 with $23,000 in subsidized loans. A total of $138,500 with $65,500 in subsidized loans are available for graduate and professional students.[20] Please remember that those numbers are subject to change and they do almost on a yearly basis.

From 1958 to the present, there have been changes, eliminations, and additions to the student aid programs. Although this program has created great problems, I am convinced that at every turn, the changes were implemented for the good of the students and the nation. Alice Rivlin, who among other things became vice chairperson of the Federal Reserve and the first head of the Congressional Budget Office, said that, "It evolved into an almost fixation—among economists anyway—with the idea that higher education added to your future income and therefore, loan finance was a sensible thing. You could pay it back out of your future income."[21]

Rivlin's remarks were emblematic of those heard all over Washington, DC, from members of Congress, policy makers, education specialists and advocates, college administrators, faculty, and others. Additionally, there were those who believed that better access and opportunity for low-income students, minorities, and women served the nation well. I happen to be one who believes that as well.

The major problem associated with this thinking and subsequent actions is the failure to provide proper oversight and appropriate fiscal controls from the beginning. Josh Mitchell, in *The Wall Street Journal* article entitled, "The Long Road to the Student Debt Crisis," said,

> The U. S. student loan system is broken. How broken? The numbers tell the story. Borrowers currently owe more than $1.7 trillion in student loans, with the average debt growing every year. Over two million of them have defaulted on their loans in just the past six years, and the number grows by 1,400 a day. After years of projecting big profits from student lending, the federal government now acknowledges that taxpayers stand to lose $31.5 billion on the program over the next decade and the losses are growing rapidly.[22]

Many other advocates are now echoing the same sentiments. Alice Rivlin, when asked in February of 2019 what she thought of the student aid system which she and others helped to create, her reply was, "We unleashed a monster."[23]

A monster indeed! Although the numbers change on a yearly basis, according to Investopedia, the average student loan debt in 2019 was approximately $37,000 with nearly 45 million borrowers.[24]

As of 2019, the debt was spread among the various programs in the following manner.[25]

20% — Federal Subsidized Loans
46% — Federal Unsubsidized Loans
12% — Parent PLUS Loans
10% — Graduate PLUS Loans
 1% — Perkins Loans
11% — Nonfederal Loans

This puts this debt second only to mortgages, but higher than auto loans and credit card debt.[26]

Given the more monstrous over $1.7 trillion student debt, the federal government has developed some avenues for relief. The Public Service Loan Forgiveness Program (PSLF) is one resource. In order to qualify, an individual must be employed by a federal, state, local, or tribal organization; 501(c)(3) not-for-profit organization; the Peace Corps; or AmeriCorps. Other organizations that are not under the Internal Revenue Code 501(c)(3) section may qualify, but requests must be made to the U.S. Department of Education for consideration.[27]

There are also other requirements for an individual receiving forgiveness from PSLF. They must be employed at least thirty hours per week at one or more 501(c)(3) organizations. Second, only Direct Loans are eligible for this loan relief, though loans from other federal programs may qualify if they are consolidated into a Direct Consolidation Loan.[28] In order to consolidate the various loans, one must know that there are provisions, caveats, and steps that must be understood and approved by the government.

Other sources of relief for students and their parents are the Higher Education Emergency Relief Fund and the Income Driven Repayment Plan. In order to seek assistance for the Higher Education Emergency Relief Fund, one must complete the Special Circumstances Form. This form is important because any financial circumstances that may have changed since the FAFSA was filed may be reported. Many parents have reported changes in their financial circumstances due to the pandemic that has gripped the world. Some have lost employment, homes, and apartments; incurred increased medical expenses; and experienced other financial strains. Therefore, it is appropriate to appeal to the institution's financial aid office by explaining the circumstances and asking for an increase in the student's financial aid package.

There are four different components to the Income Driven Repayment Plan that are designed to set the repayment of loans based on the individual's income or family size. These plans call for repayment of 10 and 15 percent of a person's discretionary income on a monthly basis. One really interesting aspect to these plans is that depending on the income and family size, there may be no monthly payment at all. Under all four plans, there is a forgiveness clause which calls for any loan balance to be forgiven at the conclusion of the repayment plan.[29]

There are other governmental proposals and plans being floated by politicians. One piece of legislation calls for the cancellation of student debt up to $50,000 for everyone whose gross income is less than $100,000. Another one proposes the forgiveness of 100 percent of student debt for all public-school teachers. Still other proposals support tuition-free college; regulation on loan servicers and for-profit colleges; and other kinds of debt relief.

It is very unlikely that these proposals will get past the Congress and be approved by the President of the United States because of the massive cost associated with funding most of these bills. Additionally, because of the highly partisan political climate that exists today in this country, many will dismiss the proposal as just one more effort to burden the taxpayers with another call for something "free," similar to those who advocate for free health care, childcare, and tuition for everyone.

Of all the options available for financing higher education, the ones dealing with student loans have proven to be the most popular forms of financing post-secondary education today. They are also the most problematic and receiving the most attention due to the sizeable amount that is owed to the federal government.

Clearly, federal student debt is out of control, but solutions must be realistic, achievable, and bipartisan. Politicians of both parties in the Congress and the Administration must shrink the political divide and work for the good of the country.

Having served as a university president for forty-four years, been appointed by both Democrat and Republican presidents to numerous federal boards and chaired several, including the President's Board of Advisors on Historically Black Colleges and Universities and the Fund for Improvement of Post-Secondary Education, I know the pressure from individuals, groups, and advocates to keep the status quo by doing nothing and "leaving things like they are." This approach is not acceptable! Therefore, I offer what hopefully are five viable recommendations for consideration.

STUDENT DEBT SOLUTIONS

My first recommendation is that the President of the United States collaborate with the majority and minority leaders in the Senate and the House and appoint a national commission to consider the suggestions as outlined here as well as any others that may be recommended. The goal is to develop realistic solutions to the massive problems associated with the current $1.7 trillion student debt. The commission must be politically bipartisan with high-level representation from the White House; the U.S. Secretary of Education; the Chairs of the U.S. House of Representatives Committee on Education and Labor; and U.S. Senate Committee on Health, Education, Labor and Pensions. Other suggested representatives could be taken from an organization such as the National Association of Student Financial Aid Administrators and include three presidents from public universities and three presidents from private universities. These are suggestions only and, obviously, there could be substitutions and/or additions.

Each representative will certainly have their own thoughts, and I would hope that there will be no "grandstanding" or political posturing. Just as in the case of COVID-19, student debt is in a crisis. Therefore, there must be no divisive politics. Politicians should stop pandering for votes because we do not need political gimmicks. We need realistic solutions.

My second recommendation deals with the interest on the loan principal that is charged to the students. Instead of charging high interest on the loans, the rate could be reduced to cover only the cost of processing. For example, in 2018–19, the U.S. Department of Education charged students 5.05 percent for the Direct, Subsidized, and Unsubsidized Loans for undergraduates, yet they only paid 2.99 percent to secure the loans from the Treasury Department. Therefore, the "add on" was 2.05 percent. In my judgment, the federal government should serve the people, not make money from the people.[30]

Third, I think that student loan origination fees should be eliminated. The National Association of Student Financial Aid Administrators has called for this elimination of fees for some time. This organization published a document in 2017 which stated that the fees amounted to some $8.3 billion from 2013–14 to 2017–18. This recommendation needs to be done now!

As discussed in the chapter on Parental Guidance, my fourth recommendation involves both the students and the federal government. For over twenty years, I have recommended that the Congress and the Administration establish a twelve- or twenty-four-month national service option for citizens ages eighteen to twenty-four. I raise the idea again in relation to the $1.6 trillion debt that is currently an albatross around our students' necks. Specifically, the Congress and the Administration could enact a law to include a provision which stipulates that after graduation from college, for every year of national service completed, one year of student debt would be forgiven. The national service could be completed in the armed services, Peace Corps, other government agencies, or approved nonprofit entities. Think about it, if a student graduated with the current average debt of approximately $36,000, some $9,000 could be eliminated upon completion of one year of national service and for twenty-four months of service, $18,000 would be eliminated. This means that in addition to the training, skills gained, and service rendered, a substantial portion of the student's debt would be forgiven.

Fifth, and perhaps most controversial, is my thinking that going forward, student loans should be awarded for the direct cost of attendance (i.e., room, board, tuition, and fees only). Currently, there are a number of students who utilize portions of their approved loans to help with car notes, support vacation travel, and in some cases send money home to help with utility and other bills. Clearly, the student loan program was not designed for this purpose.

To be sure, there will be students, parents, and advocates who complain about the loan reduction that each student will receive. Some will attempt to demagogue and/or politicize this move. In actuality, the ones who will be helped the most are the students. Upon graduation, they will not have the massive debt; therefore, the loan can be paid off sooner. This will result in a higher credit rating which will allow more and better financial flexibility in the future as they seek to acquire a home, car, or other legitimate desirables that most Americans seek.

If politicians are serious, they must cease their "pie in the sky" mentality and really get serious about a monumental problem that we have in this country. These recommendations will be a big step forward. If these recommendations were to be implemented, it would provide enormous relief to students and responsible management oversight by the federal government.

In the chapter on The College Experience, I go into some detail about the excessive amounts of money in politics today. When the United States Supreme Court decided, in a case entitled Citizens United, the federal election commission which allowed corporations, labor unions, non-profits, individuals, and other entities to spend an unlimited amount of money on politicians and political campaigns provided a major step in the assault on our democracy. Citizens United should be overturned!

This five-part plan to do something about the current more than $1.7 trillion student debt calls for students, parents, and the federal government to make and accept changes in the provisions of the current federal loan program. In order for the plan to work, everybody must give a little so that a broken system can be fixed. The biggest changes must come from members of Congress and the Administration. As difficult as this may be in our political world today, I do believe that there are enough nationally elected politicians to do what's right for the people rather than their respective parties.

All concerned must clearly understand that we cannot continue along the path that we have been traveling. Something has to be done and done now. Politicians in both parties must close the political divide that exists in this country today. Democrats and Republicans must understand the complete necessity for them to work together on this issue. I truly believe that despite the political turmoil that exists today, we can find bipartisan consensus.

CORPORATE RELIEF PROGRAMS

More and more private companies are also assisting with this massive debt by offering loan repayment assistance to their employees. Employers see the repayment assistance as a fringe benefit designed to obtain and retain quality talent. Large and small companies as diverse as Abbott Healthcare, Price Waterhouse Coopers, Penguin Random House, Fidelity Investments, CSAA Insurance Group, Nvidia, Pure Group Insurance Companies, Chegg Corporation, Staples, Zillow Real Estate Group, UNUM Insurance Company, First Republic Bank, Banfield Pet Hospital, and others have already started programs to offer assistance with student debt.

The amount and terms differ within each corporation, but are certainly welcomed by each participating employee. Although the plans are subject to change within each company, and the list of the firms is growing, some of the benefits are quite advantageous and innovative for the borrower. A sampling is listed below.

Nvidia is a technology company and a world leader in Visual Computing. It also is constantly ranked by *People Magazine* in their "50 companies that care" category. This relatively new company, founded in 1993, provides up to $30,000 in benefits for full-time workers to be used toward repayment of their student loans.[31]

Health-care company Abbott Laboratories uses quite an innovative approach in their efforts to assist with student debt as well as retirement. It will contribute 5 percent of an employee's salary toward a 401(k) retirement plan as long as the worker contributes 2 percent of their pay toward their student debt. This approach is so helpful because many relatively new employees have indicated that they could not save even a small amount toward retirement because of student debt.[32]

First Republic and Chegg offer similar benefits. First Republic is a private bank and wealth management company which offers personal and business banking, trust, and wealth management services. It caters to low-risk and high net-worth clients. Chegg is an education technology company founded in 2001, which provides high school and college student services such as textbook rentals, homework help, on-line tutorials, scholarship searches, and internship matching. Neither of these companies have a cap on the amount that they will pay in student loan repayment. First Republic will pay $1,200 for the first year, $2,000 for the second year, and $2,400 a year until the loan is paid off. Chegg provides $1,000 per year for full- and part-time workers.[33]

I anticipate that an increasing number of corporations will begin to offer loan forgiveness as a fringe benefit. As a new hire, if loan forgiveness is not mentioned, ask the human resources representative about this very positive benefit.

Going to college is an opportunity of a lifetime. It doesn't matter what major you select or the starting salary upon graduating because it basically evens out in the end. What does matter is that you take full advantage of everything that is offered.

Although the cost of higher education continues to rise, a college education can be affordable. In order to make college affordable, families must plan properly. Proper planning involves saving money and investing in 529 College Savings Plans. Students should apply for all scholarships for which they qualify at the schools they are interested in attending as well as those offered by corporations, foundations, and organizations. Federal Student Aid monies are also available to those who qualify. Though I do not recommend student loans being the primary source of funding college, loans are an option. When loans are utilized, it is important that families borrow only the amount needed. When the time comes to repay the loans, students should consider loan repayment plans like the Public Loan Service Forgiveness Program offered by the federal government as well as loan repayment benefits offered by employers. Utilizing a combination of the aforementioned strategies can make college affordable for today's students and their families.

CHAPTER V

THE COLLEGE EXPERIENCE

ENROLLMENT STATISTICS

A college education is a critical pathway for young adults not only to develop their intellectual skills, but also to heighten their social and moral responsibilities to the communities they will one day serve. Post-secondary education today is viewed by many as a rite of passage. In fact, for academic year 2020–21, there were approximately 20 million students who were enrolled in the fall semester at 4,000 institutions of higher education in the United States. According to the National Center for Education Statistics (NCES), 12 million attended full-time and 7.7 million attended part-time. Of those numbers, 16.7 million students were enrolled in undergraduate programs with 3.1 million in graduate programs. Public institutions enrolled the most students with 14.6 million, and 5.1 million in private schools. Of that 20 million, 5.8 million were in two-year institutions with 14 million enrolled in four-year institutions.[1]

Of the approximately 20 million students, 11.3 million were female and 8.5 million were male. White students enrolled slightly more than half with 10.3 million. Other racial breakdowns included 3.7 million Hispanics, 2.6 million Blacks, 1.3 million Asian and Pacific Islanders, 0.7 million of two or more races, 0.1 million

American Indian and Alaskan Native, and one million nonresident alien students. The nonresident alien students were not identified by race or ethnicity.[2]

Over three million of those enrolled are expected to be awarded degrees. Here is the anticipated categorical breakdown: 983,000 for Associate degrees; 1.9 million for Bachelor's degrees; 833,000 for Master's degrees; and 187,000 for Doctorate degrees. Although these numbers may appear high, they reflect a slight downward trend from the past. For example, in 2010 the total number enrolled was approximately 21 million while in 2019 the number was approximately 20 million.[3]

The approximately 20 million students represent a large population and reflect the fact that a large number of students, their parents, and others understand the advantages of attending institutions of higher education. There is no denying the fact that colleges are more expensive today than in the past, and the debt from borrowing to attend college is astronomical. As it relates to the $1.7 trillion student debt, I have an analysis in the chapter on Financing Higher Education Today which gives a history and a method of getting the astronomical debt under control. The college experience, however, remains an extremely positive endeavor. That judgment is formed by my college experiences.

PERSONAL COLLEGE EXPERIENCES

Attending college was not an option in my household. It was expected. Therefore, after graduation from high school at Southern Normal School in Brewton, Alabama, I began my higher education journey. I earned a bachelor's degree from Talladega College, a private Historically Black Institution; a master's degree from Virginia State University, a public Historically Black University; and a doctorate from Harvard University, a comprehensive majority university. My matriculation at all three institutions was absolutely the best!

My views and advice were not just formed by my higher educational experiences, however. Military service, family life, experiences as a teacher and executive in an anti-poverty agency, athletic participation, memberships in social organizations and a fraternity, testimony before governmental agencies, and of course, my forty-four years of service as a university president have helped to form my thoughts and opinions. The foundation for this journey was my parents, W. D. C. and Claudis Harvey.

My love for learning began early in life. It was fueled by the importance placed on education by my parents. They instilled in me a concept that I continue to subscribe to today and share with others—Education opens doors that can lead to success for those who take advantage of its opportunities. I remind students and colleagues of this often because, in my opinion, you are never too old to learn something new. This is one of the reasons that I am an avid reader. No matter where I am in the world, I read several chapters of a book, usually a novel, before bed. I strongly believe in the concept of life-long learning.

Reading has been one of the joys of my life since my parents introduced me to books at a very early age and all three institutions fed my passion. At Talladega, as freshmen, we were required to read and know something about African American, European, and Far Eastern histories as taught by Professor Margaret Montgomery. Math taught by Professors Bross and Echols, and biology taught by Professor Brown were also required. I majored in history, but took electives in art taught by Professor Driskell.

Given my desire for balance even then, I was involved in a number of other activities. My extracurricular activities included being a member of the choir my freshman year; a debater on the college debate team; an actor in the Little Theatre; and a teammate for four years on the college basketball team. I also held two jobs, including washing glasses three times a day in the cafeteria and serving in the College Snack Bar flipping hamburgers, making milk shakes, and performing other duties behind the counter as assigned by Mr. Twyman. During my four years, I had a couple of girlfriends and enjoyed playing poker with the boys. All of these experiences were wonderful!

After graduating from Talladega, I spent three years on active duty with the United States Army and was honorably discharged at Fort Lee, Virginia, on the first of February 1965. Because of my own neglect, I had not submitted an application to any graduate school;

therefore, I had to walk my unofficial transcript and discharge papers to Virginia State to meet with the academic dean. Dean Hunter read my materials, and we had a delightful conversation. Thankfully, he admitted me on the spot, conditioned on the receipt of my official transcript. After my official transcript arrived, I would get an appointment and visit with him occasionally to just chat and express my sincere gratitude for him taking a chance on me before receiving the official papers.

At Virginia State University, I majored in United States History with Dr. Edgar Toppin as my major professor. In addition to his lectures, he ignited in me the desire to write as he was the first African American that I personally knew to have authored several books. Dr. Toppin is the one who advised me to author articles in magazines and newspapers, chapters in books, and books themselves. He told me that it made no difference if others agreed with the point of view expressed, but my perspective was important and should be viewed by the public.

I did well in my studies at Virginia State, and my stay was not all academics. Because I had expressed a desire to work, Dean Hunter recommended me to be employed at minimum wage as an assistant in the Student Center. After a month on the job, the Director of the Student Center promoted me to student supervisor. My responsibilities included walking oversight of the building at night; making sure that the maintenance staff cleaned the center after closing time each night; and locking all of the doors after the staff and students had left for the night.

There was another benefit to my stay at Virginia State. I met, fell in love, and married my darling wife Norma. WHAT A BLESSING! From that union, we have three children and five grandchildren— thus far. ANOTHER BLESSING!

At Harvard University, I majored in Educational Administration and took management, business, and education courses to prepare me for a career in college administration. Professors such as Nathen Glazer, Theodore Sizer, Bernie Bruce, and Robert Binswanger were absolutely the best. Dr. Binswanger and I maintained a close professional friendship until he passed in 2019. He and Dean Sizer whetted my appetite to continue to learn and serve. Dr. Sizer was an energetic, effervescent people person. He interacted often with students, maintenance staff, secretaries, and faculty, including showing up for 3:30 afternoon tea and cookies in Rockefeller Hall. He and his wonderful wife, Nancy, also visited my wife, Norma, and me in our tiny apartment in Cambridge, Massachusetts. Both of them liked Sangria with their snacks and I would delight in fixing that drink for them. Our friendship was genuine and along with others, we were occasionally invited to their vacation home in Harvard, Massachusetts.

My Harvard years were full, exciting, educational, and wonderful! In addition to being a doctoral student, I served in a number of other roles. These included serving as Chairman of the Colloquium Board, Tutor in Adams House, Assistant Director of the Harvard Summer School in 1969, Director of the Harvard Intensive Summer Studies Program (ISSP), and Assistant to the Dean of the Graduate School of Education. My wife and I also attended Boston Celtics games at the old Boston Garden; enjoyed clam bakes in Maine, and skiing in Waterville Valley, New Hampshire. I consider all of my experiences outside of the classroom to be aspects of life-long learning.

My definition of life-long learning is the constant pursuit of knowledge for personal and professional development. I have found that people who engage in life-long learning are more informed, more socially and politically conscious, and more self-aware than others. Life-long learners appear to have the competitive edge on their jobs and tend to live more fulfilling lives. Ultimately, being a life-long learner enhances and builds upon the formal education that individuals receive during their K-12 and college experiences.

Based on my experience as a student at three institutions of higher education and my service as an administrator at Harvard, Fisk University, Tuskegee University, and Hampton University, what advice can I give to those students who are contemplating or are already matriculating at a college or university? Students should be aware that in more instances than not, many of their peers experience the same emotions (i.e., anxiety, fear, loneliness, excitement) as they do as it relates to going off to college. Stepping out of their comfort zones from environments where they were known and had established reputations can sometimes present many challenges. It is important for students to view this new experience as an opportunity rather than an issue.

This new or different opportunity should start with the setting of goals. I believe in setting long-term, short-term, mid-range, and daily goals and estimating the amount of time it will take to achieve the desired results. Give your best guess because, in most instances, you will not be precise. After doing this for a while, you will get better at your estimations.

TIME MANAGEMENT

Once you have developed your goals with approximate timelines, then you must prioritize them. The first step is to decide the order of importance of the goals that have been set for a particular time period (i.e., long-term, short-term, mid-range, or daily). In prioritizing your list, make sure that you leave a small, but requisite, amount of room for the new, unexpected, and/or general matters that invariably will come your way. Once you have made the decision to prioritize your goals and schedule, the ability to focus becomes essential.

Students must conscientiously think about developing a time management schedule. They should be aware that their regular school day is not from 8:00 a.m.–3:00 p.m. The college environment is a community that operates twenty-four hours a day. Classes are scheduled from early mornings until late evenings. The good news is that students can select their schedule of classes; however, it is most important that they realize that time management is critical to their success. Just because they schedule classes for Monday, Wednesday, and Friday only, does not mean that preparing and studying on Tuesday and Thursday can be skipped. Additionally, students must learn quickly how to manage and balance their activities. While it is tempting to get involved in many clubs and organizations because of the wide variety of programs available, it is also wise to take time and consider carefully all of the options. Students must recognize and understand their priorities early. The main goal of being in college is to continue to learn and obtain a degree. If students focus attention and time on the wrong things initially, it can delay and sometimes derail their efforts of earning a degree.

More and more colleges are seeing an increase in students coming to college with emotional baggage that can interfere with their successful matriculation. Understanding their mental health status is crucial at a time when so much change is occurring in a student's first year of college. It is important that students attend orientation activities to become familiar with all of the resources that are available to them.

Every student should keep the word "balance" in mind. There must be a healthy balance between curricula and non-curricula activities. The balance should be weighed in favor of academic pursuits, such as classes, studying, researching, and reading. Outside of the classroom, activities such as academic advising, tutorial services, peer and personal counseling, and library services are also available at most institutions. The extracurricular activities such as athletics (varsity, club, or intramural), band, choir, dance, acting, work, or partying should consume a great deal less of a student's time.

There is no set percentage for every student, but 75 percent curricula and 25 percent non-curricula is a start. College students should definitely not spend a majority of their time partying and hanging out. Too often, young folk who are away from home for the first time, without parental guidance, exercise their newfound freedom in a detrimental way. As one who has been through it, I assure you that time must be set aside for academic work and play.

As students enter into the collegiate world, they should also have an understanding that there is an expectation that they will embrace the values and standards of the institution that has elected to offer them admission. This means that students will be required to follow the rules and policies that are in place, in most instances for their very own safety and success. Students should know that there is an expectation that they have made a decision about what direction and path they want their lives to take, and in making that decision, they will exemplify all that is good and decent.

Students should know that they are entering a safe environment and that the college experience is an opportunity to grow and learn so that they develop into a productive citizen in our society. They should also know that they have a responsibility to themselves and their institution to be open to new and different philosophies and ideas. This does not mean that one must compromise their values but rather one should be respectful and mindful of people who will bring different viewpoints, different cultures, different religions, different sexual preferences, and so forth. Students must understand that the college experience is designed to prepare them for life outside of the protective walls of a collegiate environment. There will be great days and days that are not so great. Students need to know that not every day is going to be like the prospective student open houses and campus special visitation programs where everyone is happy and smiling; the food is the best; the bands are playing and the football team is winning. No—there are some days that will be difficult.

If "balance" is understood and accepted, what are the traits, characteristics, and skills that are essential to a successful college career? In addition to a strong work ethic, which has been discussed in the chapter on "Parental Guidance," there are other significant personal qualities that are needed for success. These attributes are essential, but are not exhaustive. It makes no difference if the college or university is private or public, large and comprehensive, or small liberal arts, community, trade, HBCU, Ivy League, or some other designation, it is my judgment that one of the most important traits that counts is character.

CHARACTER

Character speaks to who a person is at the core. The personal traits that people possess determine the content of their character. Building character is a life-long journey that begins early in life; it is a journey that moves slowly, one step at a time. Fortunately, it is never too late to begin the journey. You must simply choose a path. Some paths lead to good character and others lead to bad character. The good thing is that you can change directions whenever there is a need.

Since character is so important, what is it? Character is the belief in and promotion of honesty, trust, integrity, respect for self and others, gratitude, and adhering to responsible behavior. These character traits will be eminently helpful to any success that a student may have in college, in their chosen profession, and in life.

HONESTY

All of these traits of character are important, but the one that leads the list is honesty. Honesty is one of the pillars in the foundation of a good life. There are some people who will lie at the drop of a hat. Lying comes easy for them. There are even those who tell traceable lies. The really sad thing about this scenario is that in many instances the individual doing the lying doesn't know that the people he is lying to know that he is lying. To me this borders on the individual having some kind of psychosis. Often these liars get away with it because family members, friends, and close ones allow them to do so. These close ones see the good and overlook the bad. They believe in redemption and hope that the lying and misbehaving will stop. Believe me, it rarely does. If a friend, family member, fraternity brother or sorority sister, or anyone else does not tell the truth or tells a half-truth in any situation, then that person cannot be trusted. I saw a billboard once that said, "A half-truth is a whole lie." No matter how many positives can be noted in any individual, one who fails to tell the truth or fully disclose the truth cannot be counted on or trusted 100 percent. You cannot pick and choose which time, place, or situation in which you tell the truth or can be trusted.

I want people around me who are willing and able to tell the truth about any and all situations, no matter how bad or ugly the truth may be. Honest people will not fabricate information in order to cover up mistakes, avoid shame or embarrassment, or attempt to propitiate what may be a false reputation. Instead, they take responsibility for their actions, and admit when they are in error without becoming defensive, making excuses, or blaming others.

Dishonest people tell lies. On the subject of lying, President Thomas Jefferson said, "He who permits himself to tell a lie often finds it much easier to do it a second and third time, till at length it becomes habitual; he tells lies without attending to it, and truths without the world believing him. This falsehood of the tongue leads to that of the heart, and in time depraves all its good dispositions."

TRUST

To be truly counted on, an individual must tell the truth and be trusted at all times. I say often that trust is the foundation for any positive personal or professional interaction and truth is the cornerstone of trust. There is no question about the fact that trust begins with truth.

All of us have heard people say that they have many friends. This is not so! They may have a number of friendly acquaintances, but almost 100 percent of all persons can count on one hand the number of true friends that they really have. True friends are those individuals who will do anything for you and you will do anything for them. In certain vernaculars that is called a "ride or die" friend. As bad as an absence of trust can be, it has been my experience that along with being lost, trust can be regained.

If there has been a breach of trust because a mistake has been made, it should be dealt with forthrightly. I have a three-step process for those of us who make mistakes. The fact is that there is not a person alive who has not made a mistake. I know that I have. The first step is to acknowledge the mistake. The second step is to apologize for it. The third step is to endeavor not to do it again. Please know that the vast majority of people absolutely appreciate the acknowledgment of mistakes or errors. Let me give you an example of how Ebony Johnson, a student at Hampton University, dealt with a situation in a letter to me.

I want to take this opportunity to properly introduce myself since our first encounter wasn't in the most respectful manner. My name is Ebony Johnson, I am a second-year pre-nursing major from Detroit, MI. On Friday Oct. 11, 2019, I was walking out of the Student Center on my way to my statistics class when I saw you getting out of your vehicle. I wanted to greet you on that beautiful evening as the leader of our great institution. When I proceeded to speak, it didn't even occur to me at that time I didn't address you in your most rightful title and inappropriately addressed you as Harvey, completely mitigating who you are and your accomplishments. I've never felt more idiotic after that point, especially since I've worked diligently to represent Hampton University academically and socially. I've earned academic recognition on the Dean's list twice last year, completed many community service hours with various organizations, and most recently elected as the Miss Student Nursing Association and I couldn't believe I let myself mess up in such a way. Reflecting on some of the leadership skills you talk about in your book really showed me why I needed to write you this letter. I could have gone about it in a rather cowardly way and just hoped you'd forget, though that is out of my character. You talk about acknowledging what you did, taking the action to fix it, then strategically making an effort to not let it happen again. So to embody those principles and what it means to be a Hamptonian, it is with my dearest apologies to let you know how sorry I am. I truly appreciate the way in which you responded as well. You could have responded in a pejorative way, but yet you stated "That's Dr. Harvey, I am not your buddy" with a smile. I would want people to respect my accolades one day just as we should all do to you now. I admire and appreciate your leadership and hope to meet you appropriately in the near future.

This letter and the attitude of the young student is an exemplification of character. I was impressed by her sincerity and wrote the following response:

Thank you for the sincere letter of apology concerning our initial meeting outside of the Student Center on October 11, 2019, during which you addressed me as "Harvey." I appreciate you taking the time to reflect on this encounter, embrace my correction to your behavior, accept responsibility for your actions and apologize to me. This is an indication of your willingness to learn and grow as well as evidence of your maturity. I wholeheartedly accept your apology. You have impressed me with your letter. Please schedule a time with Mrs. Carolyn Acklin in my office for an appointment.

With the understanding that character counts, when contemplating the transition from high school to college, the first thing that a student should do is to look inward and ask, "What kind of person am I?" If you can with all candor answer that, "I am a decent person who possesses or strives for high-class values, standards and doing the right thing," then you are off on the right road. Please do not lie, because you are not helping yourself when you do. This admonition reminds me of the poem, "The Man in the Glass" by Dale Wimbrow.

The poem "Man in the Glass" simply says that you can fool some of the people some of the time, but you cannot fool yourself. If you lie, cheat, and steal in your interactions with others, it will eventually catch up with you. Therefore, in order to prevent the headaches and heartaches that inevitably accompany bad behavior, individuals should not attempt to mislead others for personal gain. Con artists are everywhere, but they will eventually flame out. They will find out that their short-term gain will cause them long-term pain. To the young people who are contemplating college and/or adulthood, I want you to know that your life will be better if you adhere to high standards and time-tested acceptable conduct.

INTEGRITY

One of the things that all of us must keep in mind is the importance of personal integrity. We must use our own common sense and judgment to establish how we stand on issues, instead of listening to and taking the positions of the media and politicians. We must understand that, unfortunately, politicians today seem to serve their respective parties instead of the people who elected them. The media is just as bad. In most instances the media acts more like a particular party's public relations arm with negative and personal attacks on people they don't agree with without any kind of nonpartisan filter.

Frailties of these two most important professions are more evident today than ever before. Unfortunately, that speaks volumes because our country has seen major scandals in these two areas since our beginning.

Integrity is synonymous with ethical behavior and high standards. I view it as the glue that holds these other character traits together. Integrity also means doing the right thing because it is the right thing to do. This means doing what is right, not simply what might be most popular, or expedient. When people are motivated by things other than simply what is right, their decisions are not likely the best for themselves or those around them.

While discussing integrity in the past, I have utilized two examples to illustrate the necessity for standards. The first deals with regional and national educational accrediting bodies such as the Southern Association of Colleges and Schools (SACS). These bodies have the responsibility to define and promulgate rules and regulations for every educational institution in the entire country. The accreditors have oversight over academics, finances, student life, and the like.

One such association is the Southern Association of Colleges and Schools (SACS) which has as its mission, ". . . the enhancement of education quality throughout the region and the improvement of the effectiveness of institutions by ensuring that they meet standards established by the higher education community that address the needs of society and students." The SACS region includes those institutions located in the states of Alabama, Florida, Georgia, Kentucky, Louisiana, Mississippi, North Carolina, South Carolina, Tennessee, Texas, Virginia, Latin America, and some international sites.[4] Other accrediting agencies have the same basic mission, but represent other parts of the country.

Standards are extremely important to any educational institution and adhering to those standards is taken very seriously. If, after due process, a college or university is found to be in noncompliance with standards of the association, the institution may be placed on warning or probation or lose accreditation. Losing accreditation can have a devastating effect because its students will no longer be eligible for federal financial aid.

The second example involves the National Collegiate Athletics Association (NCAA), which is the main governing body for athletics in the United States. The general principle of the NCAA is that all persons associated with the organization must act at all times with honesty and good sportsmanship. The specific purposes are as follows:

(a) To initiate, stimulate and improve intercollegiate athletics programs for student-athletes and to promote and develop educational leadership, physical fitness, athletics excellence and athletics participation as a recreational pursuit;

(b) To uphold the principle of institutional control of, and responsibility for, all intercollegiate sports in conformity with the constitution and bylaws of this Association;

(c) To encourage its members to adopt eligibility rules to comply with satisfactory standards of scholarship, sportsmanship and amateurism;

(d) To formulate, copyright and publish rules of play governing intercollegiate athletics;

(e) To preserve intercollegiate athletics records;

(f) To supervise the conduct of, and to establish eligibility standards for, regional and national athletics events under the auspices of this Association;

(g) To cooperate with other amateur athletics organizations in promoting and conducting national and international athletics events;

(h) To legislate, through bylaws or by resolutions of a Convention, upon any subject of general concern to the members related to the administration of intercollegiate athletics; and

(i) To study in general all phases of competitive intercollegiate athletics and establish standards whereby the colleges and universities of the United States can maintain their athletics programs on a high level.[5]

The NCAA also has a set of rules and regulations which all of its members must adhere to in order for its athletic teams to remain in good standing. If an individual, institution, or athletic program does not maintain the standards as outlined in the NCAA manual, they are punished or even dropped from membership. The emphasis on adhering to standards is paramount.

This is where integrity, as one of the components of character, plays such a huge role. Integrity is an integral part of good character. Standards are important because following a clearly defined set of rules is necessary if one is to have any chance of an orderly and successful life. In college or in life, no matter how much we may desire to change the rules, they are there to protect all and not just the few.

As these two examples illustrate, integrity forces individuals, organizations, and institutions to operate in an honorable manner and conduct themselves in such a way that is consistent with rules, regulations, and acceptable standards of behavior. Cutting corners does not work. Short-changing someone does not work. Attempts at deception do not work. Endeavor to be straightforward and honest at all times. This is what integrity is all about. Without a doubt, integrity should be incorporated into our academic and personal lives. When we practice integrity, we inevitably learn the meaning of respect.

RESPECT

Respect shows esteem and deference toward deserving individuals, ideas, organizations, appointed or elected positions, institutions, relationships, and the like. "Respect means that a person has and shows a high positive regard for the worth of someone or something."[6] My advice as it relates to this topic is that even if there are disagreements with someone or something, addressing the issue in a direct, straightforward, respectful manner is the appropriate way to handle the situation. People can disagree without being disagreeable. There can be debates without rancor. "Respect has great importance in everyday life. As children, we are taught (one hopes) to respect our parents, teachers and elders, school rules and traffic laws, family and cultural traditions, other people's feelings and rights, our country's flag and leaders, the truth, and people's differing opinions."[7]

It is equally important to respect oneself. Learn to appreciate one's own ability as everyone has strengths and weaknesses. One should work toward accentuating strengths and eliminating or ameliorating weaknesses. Don't be jealous of another's success. Rather, work to succeed by emphasizing the positives about oneself. This way, one's own self-esteem and self-respect are enhanced.

A positive regard for oneself can become infectious to colleagues, team members, and others with whom there is interaction. A smile can melt the largest and coldest iceberg. It can also disarm the harshest critics. Therefore, remember to always respect others as well as yourself.

In some quarters today, there are those who believe that young people do not honor integrity or adhere to standards. Additionally, there are those who believe that young people are worse today than ever before. This view can be summed up in a passage taken from a novel by John Sandford called *Bloody Genius*. In a conversation with the main character, a local businessman complained about a third of the kids today who he thought were no good. Specifically, the businessman said,

> There have always been kids who were no damn good, but now it's everywhere. EVERYWHERE. It's kids who know they're not going to be millionaires or billionaires or movie stars or famous singers or in the NBA, and it's all they want. They can't see past that. It's like they're not alive if they're not on TV. They don't want to be doctors or dentists or lawyers or businessmen; they want to be rich and famous right now. They don't want to work. All they want is to be a celebrity. Then at some point they realize it ain't gonna happen. They're not talented enough or smart enough, and they sure as shit don't want to work at getting to be famous. When they figure that out, that it ain't gonna happen, they turn mean.[8]

The novel is fiction and I hope that the characterizations are fictitious. The big problems are the influencers. One major category of influencers is some athletes with their VIP status and multimillion-dollar contracts. Beginning in junior and senior high schools, the young students want to be like these athletes with wild, unruly, and multi-color extensions in their hair; speaking and acting in a disrespectful and uncivil manner; having multiple piercings in their noses and other places; and displaying tattoos on different parts of their bodies. Appearances are important and many of these multimillionaires are not good role models. The young people see the sports and other media outlets glorifying these VIPs and they want to look, act, and be like them.

Some sports heroes and VIPs have given of themselves, their resources, time, and energy in worthwhile causes for a very long time. Many currently continue to do positive things for their communities. But, because their acts of goodwill are not covered extensively by the press, many of the young, impressionable people do not know about them. Therefore, these youngsters gravitate toward those that look like and act like thugs. They want to emulate the look and actions of those who are engaged in low-life, irresponsible, and unacceptable behavior.

Because they do not know about the good acts, many students do not want to follow the examples set by such multimillionaire superstars like LeBron James, Warrick Dunn, Kobe Bryant, and others. James' estimated net worth is $450 million, which includes endorsement compensation from such well-known companies as Nike, Coca-Cola, Intel, Kia Motors, and Verizon along with a pizza chain and a production company. His donations include some $40 million in support of over 800 children in the After-School All Stars Program in Akron, Ohio. He has also given millions in support of the Muhammad Ali Exhibit at the National Museum of African American History and Culture, the Boys and Girls Clubs of America, and his Promise School in Akron, Ohio.[9]

Warrick Dunn started a program called Homes for the Holidays in honor of his mother who was killed when he was a senior in high school. His mother was a police officer, working a second job as a security guard when this tragedy occurred. Homes for the Holidays is designed to provide housing for single-parent families who are economically disadvantaged. By the year 2018, this program in partnership with Habitat for Humanity was housing over 150 families.[10]

Kobe Bryant, who died tragically along with his daughter and seven other people, and his wife, Vanessa, supported young people and their families athletically, educationally, and culturally. They provided finances for scholarships to The Kobe Bryant Basketball Academy; youth soccer programs; a mobile health-care unit; and other unique programs to strengthen communities in the United States and abroad. Kobe and Vanessa helped engage minority kids in various enrichment experiences that have improved the lives of a number of young people. He was particularly interested in young female athletes, including his second eldest daughter who played on a basketball team he coached. Without a doubt he was just an all-around good guy.

Sports icons such as Magic Johnson, Michael Jordan, and others have also given generously to worthwhile educational and other causes. Somehow these acts of generosity and goodwill do not get the same media play that the unsavory ones do. Therefore, the K-12 students do not have the positive role models to follow.

Wouldn't it be grand if the media executives would collectively and individually promote outstanding athletes, VIPs, and others who are exhibiting good behavior and performing good deeds for our communities? Wouldn't it be grand if they were to say, "Enough is enough? My news organization is not going to glorify your athletic accomplishments if you act like a street thug in your private life." Wouldn't it be grand if these executives would teach through the power of the press some of the responsible behavior of today's talented athletes and how to deal with fame in a positive way instead of just being famous? These executives would become the force for good instead of the purveyors of decline. They would become the force to emphasize positive role models. They would become the force to promulgate and emphasize respect, self-esteem, honor, and integrity. Influencers must demonstrate the value of these traits much more.

The United States is changing at an ever-increasing pace. There is no doubt about the fact that our society has experienced some moral decay. Is it total moral bankruptcy? I do not think so and I certainly hope not. However, hope is not enough. Parents, family members, teachers, other educators, business leaders, and concerned citizens must lead, guide, teach, and promote the characteristics which enhance our society.

GRATITUDE

Gratitude is a virtue! I use this phrase many times every day. I use the phrase so often because I am thankful for the many blessings that my religious faith says that the Lord has bestowed on me. I am thankful for my parents who were simply the best; my extraordinarily wonderful wife of fifty-plus years; my children who have been an absolute joy from the day that each of the three were born; my five wonderful and precious grandchildren; my true friends (and I know who they are), who would do anything and everything for me and I for them; my formal schooling beginning in kindergarten through twelfth grade at Southern Normal School and on to Talladega College, Virginia State University, and Harvard University; the mentoring received in my higher education work experiences at Harvard, Fisk University, Tuskegee University, and now at Hampton University; the opportunity to serve as President of such an outstanding institution like Hampton; my team members at Hampton, including the seventeen individuals who went on to become presidents and CEOs of other higher educational institutions and organizations; those who helped to make Hampton University THE Standard of Excellence among postsecondary colleges and universities; my staff, past and present, in the President's Office who work day in and day out to support me and Hampton; and much, much, more.

The things listed above make me happy. When thinking about those blessings, I smile each time and thank the Lord for them. Being thankful for my many gifts has truly made my life better.

A Harvard Health paper published by the Harvard Medical School agrees with that conclusion. It states that, "With gratitude, people acknowledge the goodness in their lives."[11] The Harvard paper goes on to say that, "In positive psychology research, gratitude is strongly and consistently associated with greater happiness. Gratitude helps people feel more positive emotions, relish good experiences, improve their health, deal with adversity, and build strong relationships. People feel and express gratitude in multiple ways. They can apply it to the past (retrieving positive memories and being thankful for elements of childhood or past blessings), the present (not taking good fortune for granted as it comes), and the future (maintaining a hopeful and optimistic attitude). Regardless of the inherent or current level of someone's gratitude, it's a quality that individuals can successfully cultivate further."[12]

It is from this backdrop that I offer this guide of gratitude to those of you who are contemplating or already in college. First of all, count your blessings. By stopping to think, you probably have more to be thankful for than you realize.

Second, give thanks to those who have made your blessings possible. Remember, young people, you did not get where you are without help from someone. It may have been parents or some other family member, a teacher, neighbor, supervisor, minister, Girl or Boy Scout leader, coach, or even a stranger. Whomever they were, I want you to stop and thank them. It does not matter how small or large the favor, you should express your gratitude for the help that was received.

Thanking someone can be done verbally or in writing. I prefer both, but a letter or note on a card is better. Some call the written response a "gratitude letter." A sincere gratitude letter or card will bring joy to the recipient and a sense of satisfaction to the sender. Let me give some examples or expressions of gratitude that I received for helping some Bahamian students as a result of Hurricane Dorian.

In the chapter on "Parental Guidance," I describe in detail Hampton University's support for the University of Bahamas' students who were displaced by Hurricane Dorian. The students' performance, attitude, and gratitude have been nothing short of magnificent.

During the first semester that the Bahamian students matriculated at Hampton, I met with them on three different occasions. It was like a lovefest. They were so grateful! At each meeting, someone asked what could they do to repay Hampton University. I emphasized that the only thing that we wanted was for them to be good students, good citizens, and pay their blessings forward. The graciousness exhibited by these students is overwhelmingly wonderful! Listed below are some examples of their sincere feelings.

Coming to Hampton University after our school's campus was destroyed will forever be one of my greatest memories attached to so many emotions. One day I'll be able to "pay it forward" to someone else. We can not thank you enough Dr. Harvey. Merry Christmas.

Keishana Palmer

When I think back to my life before September 11, 2019 (the day I got accepted to HU), I remember feeling desperate to get off the Bahamas. I remember wanting to continue my education but not seeing how. Thank you for turning my desperation into not only hope, but reality. God has a special blessing for you. I know you said if I wanted to thank you, I should pay it forward. I plan to do more than that. Happy holidays!

Carneisha Demeritte

Thank you for being a beacon of light in our lives during our darkest hour. Coming to Hampton University will forever be the best thing that has happened to me. Thank you for everything! Happy Holidays!

Avia Turner

Thank you for opening the doors of Hampton University to us. Thank you for accepting us as a part of your family. We are truly appreciative of the fact that you didn't turn your back on us after we were displaced, but you saw it as an opportunity for growth and to be a blessing to us. You are impeccable. Thank you for believing in us and believing in our goals and giving us the chance to make them a reality. This experience will forever be engraved in our hearts. We appreciate you.

Shantia Dean

Think of the kind of world that we would have if more people were to reach out to others who really need help. Think also of our world if recipients would respond as graciously as these Bahamian students responded.

RESPONSIBLE PERSONAL BEHAVIOR

There is no doubt about the fact that character counts and responsible personal behavior is an integral component of character. One's behavior can be an advantage or a detriment. Those who are guilty of using illicit drugs; alcohol abuse; multiple intimate relationships; violence against the opposite sex; poor hygiene; disrespectful conduct; public disorderly behavior; lying; cheating; and stealing are scorned and no matter how they try to hide this contemptible behavior, they are eventually unmasked. In a work environment, coworkers like to be around hardworking, open, honest, trustworthy, and team-oriented people. Individuals exemplifying these traits are not only accepted, but likely to be successful on the job and rise above the rest, including earning promotions and increased salary. Judgment on the part of coworkers, supervisors, and others is not just evaluated on current behavior, but past behavior as well. This means that young college students should be very careful about their personal behavior because it can surface later on in life and prevent them from achieving much desired personal or professional goals.

Let me offer some advice. Whether or not it is fair or unfair, people determine the type of person they believe you to be based on your actions. The image that you project is the one that will follow you. An individual never gets a second chance to make a first impression. Your personal behavior, responsible or irresponsible, becomes the standard that you set for yourself and demonstrate to the world. It is very difficult to challenge one's perception of you when it is based directly upon your actions. If you present yourself to the world as being immoral, difficult, abusive, promiscuous, disrespectful, or easy to take advantage of, you will be treated as such. You should know that your behavior can and will affect every area of your life.

Responsible personal behavior seemingly is getting more difficult to achieve as both men and women are guilty of contributing to this moral degeneration and coarsening of our culture. For example, there are some men who take pleasure in boasting to their buddies about how they lie to their multiple girlfriends and, when discovered, the females get angry with each other instead of stopping the relationship with the male. Equally as egregious are first-class women who have much going for themselves except in their choice of bad boys as mates. Some of these first-class women say that they know that their actions are counterproductive, but the "bad boys" are appealing because of their outlandish behavior.

Exacerbating this abhorrent behavior are the television and movie industries along with the social media platforms that highlight and promote these negative ideals. I say to the young people that no matter where it is coming from or how many times it is viewed on the various media platforms, classless behavior is not a life form that one should attempt to emulate.

Think about the women who may attempt to relate to the women on some of the rather low-budget, risqué, and lewd television shows with their arguing, profanity-laced conversations, multiple sex partners, and paying their own way on risqué trips to resort areas with another woman's husband or boyfriend because they want intimacy, a tan, and a good time. Because some media glorify this kind of classless behavior, women in this category think that their actions are acceptable in mainstream society. Young women, IT IS NOT, and in trying to follow popular patterns, bad choices are made which may cause you to miss your season to excel.

I asked a lady who is a friend from my undergraduate days, why some young women seem to be attracted to these kinds of no-good thugs. Her response was that although she was a product of a stable, middle-class family, the bad boys she dated and the one she later married was "exciting." She said that even before she married her husband to be, "He chased every skirt that came along, but I thought that I could change him." That was her first mistake because "leopards do not change their spots." She was unsuccessful in changing him, and after a few years they were divorced. She also said that these "bad boy" types were "titillating" because they ingratiated themselves to women by offering trips to places such as Mexico, the Caribbean, or domestic resorts. Some, she said, introduced alcohol and drugs such as marijuana or cocaine in an attempt to exert control. Please understand that these types of men or women do not mean anybody any good. There is an old saying that "one can do bad all by themselves."

Some men are equally guilty of contributing to the increasing moral decay. They may want to be like the men that they hear bragging to their buddies about taking advantage of desperate women willing to spend their own money to travel and "hang out" with them for the sake of companionship. Still others may see male athletes and celebrities dressing and behaving like thugs, physically and mentally abusing their wives or girlfriends, and believe that this is what real men do. Young men, please be assured that IT IS NOT! In fact, real men don't abuse women; only cowards do. Real men don't need to rough up a woman to make themselves feel good. Unlike cowards, real men have the confidence and courage to do what is right. Real men who may be good athletes do not have babies with five or six different women in an attempt to appear macho. Real men who may be successful actors, athletes, or executives do not have ten babies by three or four different women and excuse it by saying that other women think that this kind of behavior is sexy. In fact, by degrading these women and their babies, it makes men look weak, insecure, and psychotic.

Young men, you can start to reclaim real manhood by being more respectful toward women. Fueled by some popular but thuggish-looking athletes, rap and music sensations, film, TV, and social media, I see an increasing number of young men who are exhibiting disrespectable behavior. These platforms are promulgating a growing glorification of the "bad boy" types. This translates into more young men who are comfortable in calling a woman the street name for a female dog, prostitute, or intimate relationship with their mother. This kind of language is vile and unacceptable. Would those who are guilty of this kind of behavior want someone to call their mother these kinds of names? I think not!

Too often, males and females become associated in an intimate way with individuals who do not have their best interest at heart. I heard a man say to a small group of other men that, "The young lady over there is an eagle, why is she associating with a buzzard. She is being laughed at and it makes her look bad. Doesn't she know that he has other girlfriends in the city where he works? Doesn't she know buzzards only prey on weaker animals, eat their dying or dead carcasses and then move on to another carcass?"

It is unrealistic to believe that you can change a person. Change comes from within, so you can only change yourself. You cannot stop someone from being unfaithful, abusive, disrespectful, or controlling, but you can remove yourself from such situations and not become a victim of them. Insist that your expectations are met and that your boundaries are not crossed. Have the courage and the strength to accept nothing less than what you deserve in your personal relationships.

Young people, please understand that a girlfriend, boyfriend, or a mate who is seeing and servicing others can cause immeasurable harm both mentally and physically to themselves and others. Anybody who seeks only companionship or a good time with a particular individual who has multiple other intimate friends is guaranteeing themselves many future heartaches.

When making decisions on who to date or marry, it is important to make sure that your values align with each other. Does this person have good personal behavior? Do they have goals and aspirations? Do you have similar views and experiences? All of this matters and will ultimately play a role in the relationship.

It is also important to set expectations as to how you want to be treated and boundaries for what you will and will not accept. If a person mistreats you once, more than likely such mistreatment will be a pattern in the relationship. If they cross the line once, and there are no consequences, they will cross the same line again and probably go a little further.

Although not a panacea, possessing and practicing good character traits of truth, trust, integrity, respect for themselves and others, and responsible personal behavior are exceedingly important for personal and professional success and cannot be stressed enough. Good character is the glue that holds families, relationships, organizations, and nations together. When we are not of good character, even though we may not realize it, we diminish ourselves as individuals.

CHAPTER VI

SIGNIFICANT LIFE SKILLS FOR SUCCESS

The character traits discussed in the previous chapter are essential ingredients to a life well-lived. They, however, are not the only personal qualities and life skills that young students and others should seek as keys to their success and significance. Some other qualities are listening, discipline, loyalty, perseverance, and civility. These qualities along with the character traits of honesty, integrity, respect, trustworthiness, and responsible personal behavior are life skills which will lead to success in one's personal and professional lives.

LISTENING

Listening almost seems to be a lost commodity in today's world. Political parties, nations, and individuals develop their own thoughts about a subject, policy, themselves, or another person, and for some it is difficult to view things in an objective manner. This is true because a great deal of the time no one wants to listen to another point of view. Their mind is made up and they do not want to be confused with facts.

One has to look no further than our nation's capital. The political climate is toxic, and there is little civility between the political parties. This chasm is exasperated with the twenty-four-hour, seven-days-a-week news cycle. It is poisoning our country. Those on the left of the political spectrum believe that they are right and those on the right believe the same thing. What has resulted is almost a complete lack of civil discourse and compromise. There was a time when the two major party candidates would fight extremely hard to get elected, and once elected, the representatives would govern for the people. Now, it seems that they only govern for the party. The bosses in each party control the narrative, the vote, and the outcome.

My hope is that this generation of young people will reverse this trend. One way to do this is for those who are preparing for college or already in college to organize a "movement" with a goal of reducing the major problem of incivility in the country by holding the chief culprits accountable. Even if this movement does not take place, we must eliminate the divide. Although there are flaws, the United States is the greatest country on earth! We need to be more civil even if we disagree with other views. Remember, we can disagree without being disagreeable!

Clearly politicians and their supporters should listen more and talk less. There is an old adage which states that a person has two ears and one mouth. Therefore, they should listen twice as much as they speak. Many people do not listen for perhaps a myriad of reasons. They may be immature, temperamental, neurotic, stubborn, or narcissistic. They may also think that they have all the answers or are ashamed of the information that is being presented. Others may simply have an unwarranted sense of independence or be socially, personally, and/or professionally incapable of adhering to what is being passed on to them. If anyone does not listen and they fit into any of the above categories, they should attempt to overcome what I believe is a detrimental malady.

Although applicable to everyone, listening is particularly advantageous to students who are in college. Young people, I say that you should listen carefully to what your parents, guardians, mentors, professors, and others impart to you. If these people have demonstrated that they have your best interest at heart, why listen to others who probably have a selfish motive? It continues to amaze me that there are those who adhere to the directions and actions of self-serving members of the opposite sex, so-called friends and acquaintances whose beliefs and actions are often contrary to the advice and direction of those who have truly been there for them in times past. This kind of decision-making is usually not a good step in building a good, lasting relationship. As a matter of fact, it usually ends badly.

Some have asked me, "How can I become a more effective listener?" My answer is a simple one. "Keep your mouth shut, your mind open, do not interrupt until the point is made, and then evaluate what has been said before you act." I have also suggested that if the emotions are too high at the moment, one should go to a quiet place and spend some quality time evaluating what has been expressed.

Being an effective listener is important in any interaction with others. This is so because it enhances learning in academic settings, the professional workplace, and in personal relationships.

In academic settings, students must listen intently in classrooms, lecture halls, and tutorial sessions. It is in these settings where intelligence is acquired, instructions are given, reading assignments are made, and problems are discussed and solved.

In work situations, instructions are disseminated relating to tasks that must be performed. Supervisors explain the culture of the particular company which they would like all employees to follow. Values are articulated. Goals, objectives, and strategies are outlined. Priorities and the employees' role in achieving them are also discussed. None of these tasks can be achieved without attentive listening.

Despite the vagaries of society today, there is no substitute for effective and discerning listening. As a college student, you cannot learn without listening. You cannot grow intellectually without listening. You cannot be a good wife, husband, mother, father, sister, brother, or friend without being a good listener. You cannot be a responsible citizen without listening. Therefore, if you want to be a good student and citizen of the world, please strive to listen more and listen better.

In personal relationships, listening, along with observing behavior, allows one to be aware of the other person's words, deeds, and intentions. Be aware that words alone do not portray the whole story.

By listening to the words and observing the facial and body language, one is better able to discern the substance and sincerity of the message. Some men and women are very adept at deceiving and obfuscation. In today's world, one must be extra careful about what is being said and heard.

DISCIPLINE

One of the necessary elements of student success is discipline. Phrases such as "controlled behavior," "self-control," and "willpower" come to mind when I think of discipline. Having a degree of discipline is extremely important for all people, but even more so for college students. First and foremost, students must exercise discipline in the pursuit of their academic goals and objectives. This means spending appropriate time studying, attending classes, completing required papers, reading for fun and enjoyment, and balancing extracurricular activities.

Being disciplined also means saying no to distractions. A distraction is anything or anyone that shifts your focus from the task at hand or alters in a negative way the plan that you have established and the goals that you have set to make your vision a reality. Such distractions can come in the form of temptations, people, ideas, or events. It is important to note that you may be your own distraction when you engage in activities that do not keep you on track to reach your goals. These distractions could come in the form of drugs, alcohol, vaping, opioids, over-eating, and too much screen time on social and other media.

Appropriate balance is a necessity because of the many and various forms of temptations in our society today. Some of these temptations relate to drugs, alcohol, eating habits, inappropriate time spent on video games and other social media platforms, too much socializing, or a myriad of other things. Many students are away from home and parental oversight for the first time; therefore, they must possess or acquire the self-discipline to overcome these temptations.

Drugs are the most pervasive temptation and distraction to avoid at all costs. I firmly believe that drugs are the scourge of the earth. Using drugs, associating with drug dealers, or running with a crowd that does drugs will either cause your life to be miserable or kill you. My strong advice is to stay away from narcotics such as marijuana, heroin, cocaine, morphine, opium, and other addictive substances. The same can be said of methamphetamines. It has been reported that more and more young people are turning to methamphetamines which has resulted in an increase in deaths associated with this narcotic. One reason for this surge may be that according to the United States Drug Enforcement Administration, methamphetamines from Mexico are being brought across the Southern border in record numbers and they are cheap.[1]

As if the above-mentioned drugs are not enough of a clear and present danger to our society, two other categories of harm have reached crisis proportions. These are vaping from electric cigarettes or e-cigarettes and opioids, which are causing, in some cases, death, illnesses, and injuries. Unfortunately, the use of vaping is on the rise. In 2019, the CDC said that some 5.4 million students in middle and high school used e-cigarettes.[2] In an article by Linda Richter, Director of Policy Research and Analysis at the Center on Addiction, vaping was described as "... the act of inhaling and exhaling the aerosol, often referred to as vapor, which is produced by an e-cigarette or similar device. The term is used because e-cigarettes do not produce tobacco smoke, but rather an aerosol, often mistaken for water vapor, that actually consists of fine particles. Many of these particles contain varying amounts of toxic chemicals, which have been linked to cancer, as well as respiratory and heart disease."[3]

Other concerns as expressed by the Food and Drug Administration (FDA) and other health-care agencies are seizures related to nicotine poisoning; explosions with the devices used in vaping; and lung injuries and disease associated with vaping. In an article entitled, "Everything You Wanted to Know About The Vaping Health Crisis," Mary Beth Griggs noted that the FDA had received 127 reports about "seizures or other neurological symptoms" and "exploding e-cigarettes." In the same article, Dr. Griggs indicated that the Centers for Disease Control and Prevention (CDC) "has identified 2,172 probable cases" of lung injuries in forty-nine states, the District of Columbia, and the U.S. Virgin Islands. Alaska has not reported any cases as of yet.[4] Please note that when the CDC uses the phrase "probable cases" as the cause of this significant increase in lung injury and disease this fact has not been definitively linked to vaping. There is suspicion, but no specific confirmation. What has been confirmed is the FDA's warning to the public not to use e-cigarettes containing tetrahydrocannabinol (THC). THC is the substance in marijuana that makes its users high.[5]

There have also been concerns expressed about the devices themselves which are utilized in vaping. The devices are usually made of plastic and metal with a cartridge for the e-liquids, a heating component, and a mouthpiece. The liquids may have a vegetable base with nicotine or some other substance. One of the extremely popular products is called JUUL which looks like a USB flash drive. According to Dr. Richter, it has almost three-fourths of the current vaping market share. Its popularity comes from the fruity and good tasting flavors that are used in the liquid makeup. One real danger in JUUL is that some of its flavor pods may have about as much nicotine as a pack of cigarettes.[6]

Another real concern is the fact that some heating components in these devices have exploded and shattered jaws or even caused death.[7] The FDA believes that these explosions may be battery related. Others have speculated that the cause may be the chemicals that change when heated. A study in the *Tobacco Control Journal* estimated that there were some 2,035 e-cigarette explosions and burn-related injuries from 2015 until 2017.[8]

Warnings against e-cigarettes and vaping are coming from a number of quarters. The United States Surgeon General in November 2019 called youth vaping an epidemic. In 2018, the Surgeon General spoke with concern about the high content of nicotine in JUUL. President Trump had indicated that all e-cigarettes be banned and the states of Michigan and New York banned flavored vapes in the summer of 2019. Massachusetts banned all e-cigarettes and California mounted a campaign against counterfeit and black-market products. Some corporations like Walmart have become concerned enough to cease the sale of e-cigarettes, and Apple Corporation has removed all apps related to vaping from its App Store.[9] A study done by the University of Michigan and reported by Higher Education revealed that "... the use of vaping products or e-cigarettes, to vape marijuana as well as nicotine, doubled between 2017 and 2018."[10]

Young people, although nothing definitive has been scientifically proven against vaping yet, it would be wise to take a hard look at what is being said. Vaping can increase heart disease; increase the risk of exposure to toxic chemicals and harmful metals; cause formaldehyde chemicals to be released in your body; cause permanent lung damage and disease; and introduce the highly addictive nicotine into your body. If only one or two of these claims is true, why subject your body and your future to this kind of agony and pain?

The American Lung Association's view on this matter is unequivocal. Their statement says, "E-cigarettes are not safe and can cause irreversible lung damage and lung disease." The president of this association goes further by saying, "No one should use e-cigarettes or any other tobacco product."[11]

Opioids are different because they are prescribed drugs. However, they may be even more dangerous. These are prescribed for severe pain and include such drugs as OxyContin, Codeine, and Vicodin. Opioids also include heroin, synthetic drug fentanyl, morphine, and others. The legal and illegal drugs in this category are known to be highly addictive. Fentanyl, for example, has been reported as being eighty to one hundred times stronger than morphine. As if this fact is not bad enough, some drug dealers have increased its potency by adding it to heroin. The combination of fentanyl and heroin is so powerful that many of its users die from overdoses. The Centers for Disease Control and Prevention reported that opioids were responsible for over 70% of drug overdose deaths in 2019. Seventy-two percent of these deaths involved synthetic opioids.[12]

The usage of opioids has reached epidemic proportions in our country and on some college campuses. The National Institute on Drug Abuse estimated that there were more than 30,000 deaths associated with opioid abuse between 2002 and 2015.[13] The Centers for Disease Control and Prevention (CDC) indicated that the overdose rate among teens actually doubled from 1999 to 2015.[14] Extending their survey by two years, the CDC also reported that from 1999–2017, drug overdose deaths totaled more than 702,000 with over 400,000 attributed to opioids. In 2017 alone the drug over-dose deaths exceeded 70,000 people with approximately 68 percent or 47,600 attributed to opioids. Interestingly enough, the states with the most deaths to overdose ratio were, "West Virginia (57.8 per 100,000), Ohio (46.3 per 100,000), Pennsylvania (44.3 per 100,000), District of Columbia (44.0 per 100,000), and Kentucky (37.2 per 100,000).[15]

One good bit of news is that according to the CDC, there was a decline in drug overdose deaths in 2018. The 67,367 drug over-dose deaths represented a 4.1 percent decline from the previous year. Included in this reduction were fourteen states and the District of Columbia. Unfortunately, there were higher death rates in the states of California, Delaware, Missouri, New Jersey, and South Carolina. The really sad statistic is a 10 percent increase in deaths involving synthetic opioids from 2017–18.[16] As one can see, we continue to have a major problem with opioids.

These statistics are alarming and involve more than teenag-ers and young adults. Some physicians and pharmacists have been accused of overprescribing and selling these opioids. A number of companies in the drug industry, including "drug makers, distributors and retail pharmacies are facing lawsuits from virtually every state and thousands of city and county governments."[17] With over 2,000 lawsuits already filed, a few have been settled. A generic maker of drugs from Staines-upon-Thames, England, has settled lawsuits val-ued at $1.8 billion with forty-seven attorneys general in forty-seven states and territories. This drug maker was one of the highest producers of opioids in the entire United States. An $18 billion attempt at a settlement by three large wholesalers was not accepted by twenty state attorneys general.[18] Because of the pain, distress, suf-fering, and deaths that have occurred as a result of the alleged over-prescribing, irresponsible marketing, and sloppy industry oversight, any settlement will probably be in the excess of $100 billion.

The drug naloxone has been identified as an agent that can save lives because it can reverse an opioid overdose. The National Institute on Drug Abuse has recommended naloxone as being safe and can be used by individuals other than medical personnel in an emergency.

For this reason, some colleges have begun to keep naloxone in stock in the event that it is needed.

My advice to those of you who are anticipating going to college and to those who are already in college is to stay away from opioids and vaping. As it relates to opioids, you do not need to pop a pill every time you have some pain. Headaches, cramps, joint pain, or other minor pains do not require opioids.

Even some surgeries do not require this kind of medicine, unless the pain is unbearable. I can use myself as an example. After one of my surgeries, the physician prescribed an opioid (Percocet) with the admonition that I did not need to take the medicine unless the pain reached a level of five on a scale of zero to ten. Although I had major surgery (a complete knee replacement), my pain level never reached a level of five. Therefore, I did not take even one pill.

I have spent a lot of time discussing the hazards of illegal and legal drugs because as stated earlier, drugs are the scourge of the earth. Whatever pleasures they may bring are not worth the pain and distractions which accompanies them. Avoiding as many distractions as possible which interfere with the main goal of the promotion of learning at the higher educational level is strongly advisable. Clearly, the use of drugs of any kind, including opioids, vaping, and e-cigarettes could be a major stumbling block toward the attainment of a college degree.

As a university president, I have seen young, promising students become distracted to the point of destruction as a result of their involvement with drugs, vaping, or opioids. At Hampton, we have a no tolerance policy for drugs. We share this information with parents and students early on in the application process. There is even a popular phrase on campus that says, "If you are caught with drugs by nine a.m., you will be out by five p.m." Despite being fully aware of the policy and the associated consequences, there are those students who take the risk of using drugs. As a result, several students have been caught with drugs and expelled from school. Some of those expelled have even been graduating seniors who violated the policy within days of graduating.

Being expelled from school is a major distraction on a college student's path to success. Even if they plan to attend another university, the expulsion is on their record and might possibly hinder them from being accepted elsewhere. In my opinion, the distraction of a few moments of drug-induced euphoria is not worth throwing your life's plan off course, even only temporarily.

You should avoid distractions at all costs, but it would be unrealistic to believe that you will go through life without any. Therefore, when distractions do occur, it is best to get back on track as soon as possible. Never abandon the vision. Do whatever it takes to regain your focus and continue to persevere.

Alcohol abuse is another vice that can derail our future plans. Perhaps it is unrealistic to suggest that one should completely avoid alcohol given the many off-campus social events that college students attend where alcohol is served. My advice, however, is to approach this temptation with caution. Alcohol abuse can have devastating consequences for anyone. I am aware of situations where students have been transported to the hospital because of an overindulgence of alcohol which resulted in alcohol poisoning. There are other reported incidents of Greek Letter organizations throwing parties where potential members and pledgees have been hospitalized or died from overdoses of alcohol. In this regard, a number of colleges and universities have suspended these Greek Letter organizations for multiple years or indefinitely.

As suggested, avoidance of alcohol may be unrealistic, but moderation is not. I cannot prescribe the number of drinks that an individual should take, but if anyone feels themselves getting slightly inebriated or high, they should cease their alcohol intake. Stay at the club, bar, or party if you wish, but drink a soft drink or water instead. Not only can inebriation create physical harm, it can also lead to unwanted sexual activity, including rape.

Another temptation to watch out for may be overeating or simply consuming too many sweets. Medical newsletters and journals from medical facilities such as the Mayo Clinic, Cleveland Clinic, Harvard Medical School, and UCLA Medical School have advised that sugar can be harmful to our health. An overindulgence in sweets can result in weight gain, cardiovascular diseases, diabetes, or other medical maladies. Fatty foods can be detrimental. Certain kinds of meats can cause digestive problems. Some people may not know it, but they are addicted to that "must have" morning latte or that extra pie or cake. The addiction could be that tasty candy bar or soft drink.

Whatever food or drink it may be, we should acknowledge our weaknesses. Too many do not acknowledge the problem or make excuses for their overindulgence. I was told once that excuses are the tools of incompetence.

Discipline is desperately needed in self-regulating the amount of time that some young people spend on the various social media platforms. There are reported instances of students all over the country skipping not only classes, but meals as well because they are so enthralled with what is on social media, including the many games available for them to play; porno sites; current events; engaging with other young people; commercial advertisements; and the like. Because these sites are not regulated, much of what is shown is not accurate. The hate groups, mentally imbalanced individuals, political operatives on the left and right, foreign entities, and others have equal access, as long as they pay the required fees. This means that instead of engaging in a more well-rounded college life of curricular and extracurricular pursuits, the student is being short-changed by spending an inordinate amount of time on these platforms which, in a number of instances, present a distorted view of reality. Remember, moderation and balance are the keys in dealing with these temptations.

Much research has been conducted on the amount of time people spend on their electronic devices. Time spent in this manner is called "screen time." Some of the research indicates that having too much screen time can negatively affect children, teens, and adults. Therefore, researchers recommend that parents monitor their children's screen time and restrict their access to certain information. In addition, they suggest that parents monitor their own screen time and be aware of the behaviors that they are modeling as it relates to technology use.[19]

What can those of us who are parents, family members, teachers, or administrators do to assist in the development of self-discipline? First of all, we must help in identifying the particular problem. If it is indulging in any of the temptations listed above or others, we should work with the individuals, in a non-adversarial way, to help them change their ways. If we find ourselves lacking self-discipline, it is important to connect with others who can assist us in making improvements as well as hold us accountable.

For example, suppose that the issue is overspending on a routine basis. Ask the individual to set aside a time when you might discuss budgeting by analyzing the expenses and revenues. Look at all of the income, including scholarships, loans, work study jobs, and parental support. Put that on one side of the sheet. Then look at all of the expenses. Be sure to include on the expense side a line item for "fun" activities such as an occasional movie, lunch, dinner, hair upkeep for men and women, makeup for women, or a new item of clothing. A budget might look like the hypothetical one listed below.

The average cost for students to attend college today is $40,000 per year, although that cost is much higher at some institutions and lower at others. Below is a hypothetical budget based on national averages. For example, the national average for parental contributions is 43 percent.

Budget

Revenue			Expenses		
Scholarship	12,000		Tuition	25,000	
Parental Support	15,500		Room & Board	12,500	
Federal Grants	4,000		Books & Supplies	1,000	
Private Grants	2,500		Comprehensive Fees	2,900	
Work Study	1,800		Technology Fees	250	
Loans	8,000		Cable	190	
			Personal Expense & Fun	1,800	
	Totals	43,800		Totals	43,640

As one can see from this hypothetical budget, the revenues are greater than the expenses, even with the "fun" money included. If for any reason all of the excess funds are not spent in any given month that money should be placed in a savings or holding account at the institution or at a local financial institution for any future expenses.

Now that the facts are before the individual, the trick is for that person to be disciplined enough to stay within the budget. One cannot overspend in the "fun" category one month and say that the difference can be made up in some subsequent month. Usually, these funds are never made up and the individual is on a downward spiral again.

If for any reason the budget is busted, sit down with an advisor or by oneself and devise a plan to rectify the situation. Identify realistically where you went wrong and endeavor not to make that mistake again. Do not beat yourself up about not achieving your desired goal, but resolve to be successful in the future. Making changes in either the revenue or expense side of this hypothetical budget is permissible. Just do not lose sight of your goals and the steps necessary to achieve them.

LOYALTY

Loyalty is a highly desirable quality characterized as being reliable, trustworthy, committed, and faithful to an individual, group, family, institution, organization, nation/state, cause, religion, or the like. The concept of loyalty is not new. It has been expected and demonstrated throughout history. Although the motivation was not always positive. The ancient Greeks and Romans required it. Under penalty of death, some dictatorial regimes have demanded it. The Germans, during the Nazi era, insisted upon it. Kings, queens, lords, and others in positions of power have ordered it. Even today, there are some totalitarian regimes that command it.

As it relates to desirable life skills relative to success in college and beyond, I will discuss the relationship between loyalty and institutions of higher education. There are three main constituent groups associated with colleges and universities that place a significant emphasis on loyalty. These are the individuals who work at the institutions, those who matriculate at them, and those who earn their degrees from them.

Since my work experiences have primarily been at institutions of higher education, I can only comment or derive my observations from the time I have spent on these campuses. At each institution, I worked with some of the most dedicated and loyal faculty, staff, and administrators that I ever imagined existed. Working at a college or university is not just a job for most, but a way of life. It is difficult to work in an environment that is also a living community and not develop a connection beyond that typical 9–5 workday. I have worked with persons who on a daily basis go well above and beyond the call of duty because of their loyalty to the institutions. These individuals embrace the mission, standards, and goals, and then work tirelessly to ensure that everything associated with the institution is top-notch or first-rate.

The second group of individuals that exemplifies the characteristics of loyalty is students. When students attend college, the institution often becomes their home away from home and they gain a new family. Once there, they are embraced by faculty, staff, alumni, and other students and a bond is formed. The more they learn about their institution of choice, the more committed they become to its mission, goals, programs, and projects. The students are the lifeline of an institution and their loyalty to it is a reflection of the great work being done there. No institution is perfect, so students' loyalty should not shift based on small complaints like "I don't like the food in the cafeteria" or "My dorm room is not big enough." Even an issue with a particular faculty or staff member should not cause students to become disloyal to the institutions that nurture them and provide them with an education. The fact that you applied to the institution, were accepted, and matriculated is reason enough to be a proud and loyal supporter. When students are proud of their institution, they brag about it to others. This bragging often becomes a friendly competition that sometimes elevates to rivalry status. Upon graduation, this loyalty is demonstrated in former students' support for their institution as alumni. For those of you heading to college, I encourage you to commit yourself to being loyal to your institution and being a positive representation of it. Many people do not realize that when they disparage their institution, they discredit themselves and their degrees.

The alumni are the third group of individuals who exemplify loyalty. When individuals have strong feelings of support and allegiance to something or someone, they demonstrate this through loyalty. Hampton University has one of the most engaged and supportive alumni associations with which I have been affiliated. Hampton alumni work tirelessly, individually, and collectively, to support the institution. From the National Hampton Alumni Association

(NHAA, Inc.) to regional and local chapters, the alumni have been loyal since its beginning. Some of the evidence of their loyalty is the millions of dollars raised to provide scholarships for students as well as the assistance they provide each year to ensure that we recruit the best and the brightest students from across the country. Alumni support in word and deed is critical to the success of an institution. Those of you who have graduated, I encourage you to demonstrate your loyalty to your alma mater by giving of your time, talent, and treasure. Do not try and make policy or run the institution as that is not the purpose of an alumni association or an alumnus.

Loyalty touches all of our lives. However, loyalty that is demanded is not true loyalty. True loyalty is a choice one makes. The loyalty that we have toward individuals and entities is based on our belief in them, their actions, and their commitment to us. In other words, loyalty is a two-way street. When demonstrating your loyalty to others, be sure that they deserve it. Ask yourself, "Are these individuals reliable and trustworthy? Are they as committed, obedient, and faithful to me as I am to them? Can I count on them to support and defend me when necessary?" If you can answer yes to these questions, then you have identified those who are worthy of your loyalty.

As I ponder the concept of personal loyalty, I consider it to be one of the most important actions that one human can exhibit toward another. Persons who are loyal to another person tend to do so because they respect and honor the character of that person. Typically, it is because the individual is trustworthy, faithful, supportive, and caring. When one conducts their personal and professional life in this manner, they will always have loyal supporters. While it may be "nice" to think that you have a large number of friends, the fact is that anyone can count on one hand the number of true friends. I personally would rather have a handful of "loyal" friends who have my back and know in their hearts that I have theirs.

PERSEVERANCE

Perseverance is important because most, if not all of us, have goals, objectives, and dreams. They may be small ones or seemingly impossible ones. Perseverance is keeping those goals in front of us and not giving up. Sometimes when our dreams do not become a reality immediately, we give up. This we should not do, and perseverance will aid us in achieving our goals.

As I have said in other places in this book, we should develop a plan to accomplish our desired outcome once a goal, objective, or dream is formulated. Our outcome could also include options. For example, suppose as a college senior you are interested in attending medical, law, or graduate school. My advice is the same that I offered in the chapter on Preparing for College. Apply to several colleges or universities including colleges that you are reasonably sure will accept you. Others could be to those that you are not sure will respond positively. Some can be to those institutions that you do not feel will accept your application. The results may surprise you.

I have served on admission committees at several institutions and although the committee members are not usually biased, they are not always objective. Even though all of the admissible candidates must meet minimum qualifications, admission committee members may take a special interest in a particular candidate for a special reason. That reason could be leadership experience; singing or acting talent; research interest; published articles; athletic prowess; or a multiplicity of other things. Even if a few of the institutions reject you, think of the elation when one or more accepts you. Even if all of them reject you, do not give up. Select others and repeat the process. Quitting is never an option to a desired goal.

Remember, perseverance is the persistence and tenacity not to quit, even if there are those urging you to do so. Unfortunately, there are always people who want you to fail, or try to bring you down. They will rumor, gossip, or lie to you. The source of this psychosis comes in all shapes, sizes, professions, colors, and genders. They may be avowed enemies, friends, classmates, sorority sisters, fraternity brothers, disgruntled associates, mentally challenged persons, or individuals who are just jealous for no reason. In no instance should you attempt to placate this evilness. Most of these types of people are miserable human beings and just do not like the fact that you are not as demented as them. Denzel Washington was quoted as having said,

"Some people will never like you because your spirit irritates their demons." His comment is so true!

I call these people "snakes." My response to snakes is that they do not like heights; therefore, I just keep on climbing. I urge each student reading this passage to do the same thing.

A perfect example of someone who persevered is the late actor Chadwick Boseman who had a short, but impactful, cinematic career. Boseman's first acting job was on the soap opera *All My Children*. He held the job for only two days. On his first day of work, he questioned the stereotypical nature of his character as a Black thug. He had decided that he did not want to play roles that presented Blacks in a negative light. On his second day of work, they replaced him. This, however, did not deter Boseman who was deeply committed to his cause. He continued to seek roles that presented positive images of Blacks.

Although he made many television appearances before shifting his talents to the big screen, most consider Boseman's breakout role his portrayal of the baseball legend Jackie Robinson in the film *42*. He later went on to portray James Brown in *Get on Up* and Thurgood Marshall in *Marshall*. Boseman's name became synonymous with playing real-life Black heroes. Then, his career took a major turn when Marvel Studios cast him in *Captain America: Civil War* as T'challa the Black Panther, one of the first Black superheroes in Marvel Comics.

Boseman reprised this role in the groundbreaking movie *Black Panther*, the only movie ever dedicated to a Black superhero, and one of the highest grossing films in history. Featuring a majority Black cast and directed by a Black man, the movie was a box office and critical success. His character was the ultimate representation of the positive image of Blacks that Boseman wanted to portray. *Black Panther* became a movement, and Black people everywhere felt empowered by it, especially young children. Black Panther dolls, posters, costumes, T-shirts, and other paraphernalia was in high demand. Later, Boseman appeared as Black Panther in both the *Avengers: Infinity War* and *Avengers: Endgame* movies. The writing of the script of *Black Panther: Wakanda Forever* began shortly before Boseman's unexpected death in 2020.

When Boseman died of colon cancer at the age of forty-three, the world was in shock. Very few people, even those with whom he had worked extensively, knew that he had been diagnosed with the disease in 2016. In a statement, his family shared that many of the movies for which he was best known were filmed in-between his surgeries and chemo treatments that he hoped might eradicate the disease. This revelation made his work even more powerful and impactful.

Just imagine Boseman spending long hours on sets, learning his lines, performing stunts, and delivering take after take while his body was suffering. This, dear reader, is what I call perseverance. He never shared what he was going through. He did not allow the disease to become a distraction, acting in numerous films while fighting cancer. Instead, he remained focused on his vision of portraying positive Black images on film for the world to see. He followed his vision until the end of his life. His work will stand for generations to come.

Personally, I believe that Boseman's vision, work ethic, time management, discipline, ability to avoid distractions, and perseverance had a little something to do with him being a graduate of an HBCU. He delivered a commencement address in 2018 at his alma mater, Howard University—the other HU—in which he talked about the impact that the school had on his career. That same year, Ruth Carter delivered the commencement at her alma mater, Hampton University—the REAL HU—in which she challenged the graduates to "create a place for yourself in this ever-changing world."

Now, I'm sure you're wondering why I mentioned Ruth Carter in the discussion of Chadwick Boseman. Well, there is a good reason for this. Boseman and Carter worked together on *Black Panther*, both receiving critical acclaim and winning numerous awards. Boseman was the out-front King of Wakanda and Carter was the behind-the-scenes queen who dressed him and the entire cast in their magnificent attire. Carter's work as costume designer on *Black Panther* garnered her an Academy Award for Best Costume Design, and she was the first Black woman to receive the award. She also earned a star on the Hollywood Walk of Fame. These two HBCU graduates were key players in a film that changed the movie industry! They are living examples of how far an HBCU education can propel you when you take the HBCU experience to heart. This level of success was a result of them persevering!

Often, college students are faced with challenges during their matriculation. These challenges may be academic, social, familial, personal, or health-related. When these situations occur, some students choose to take a break from school with the intention of returning later while others leave school and give-up all together. Other students meet these challenges head-on and remain enrolled in an effort to persevere and make their dreams of receiving a skill and a college degree a reality.

One should understand that there are times when incidents and situations will occur during a college student's matriculation that impact their college experience. In some instances, a student may have no control over these situations. The crisis may come in the form of a global, national, state, or local occurrence; or it may come as some type of a disruption of campus life. No matter the crisis, college students are put in a position where they must cope with the crisis and manage whatever change it requires of them. This is not always an easy task.

One such occurrence was the worldwide COVID-19 health pandemic. As of March 2021, the virus had affected over 120 million individuals worldwide with 2.55 million deaths and more than 28.7 million cases in the United States with approximately 516,000 deaths. The economy was also dealt a devastating blow. Our nation's economy from mid-March through June lost approximately $350–450 billion per month. Between March and July over 140,000 businesses had closed. In the month of May 2020 alone, there was a 48 percent increase in bankruptcy filings over May 2019.[20]

Colleges and universities also felt the blow of the chaos and confusion. Almost all of them canceled in-person instruction in favor of remote instruction. This move created problems with a few institutions because some professors were not comfortable in delivering their course content remotely and in other instances the technology itself was not the best. Many of these institutions have reported an annualized financial loss of $75–100 million and more due to obligatory contracts and the absence of revenue associated with tuition, room, board, athletics, and retrenchment of personnel.

When the pandemic hit, higher educational institutions and their leaders responded differently. Some continued remote instruction only. Others instituted a hybrid model of in-person and remote. Still others returned solely to on-campus delivery of course content. The same could be said for athletics. Some conferences and institutions canceled fall sports including football, while others continued to play an abbreviated schedule. At Hampton, we asked ourselves a very simple question as it related to reopening in the fall. Since the virus was spiking in a number of states where our students resided, the question was, "Is it safe?" The answer for us was a resounding "No." Therefore, for Fall 2020, Hampton University offered remote instruction only.

Something of this magnitude obviously created an unprecedented situation for students. They were required to vacate their campuses as a health and safety measure. Instead of going to classes, attending athletic contests, socializing with friends, or just "hanging-out on campus," they were required to spend their time at home. In many instances, "home" was in a state that was under a "Stay at Home" order by their respective governors. Not only did this create tension within families, but it brought about and/or exacerbated stress and trauma, along with other kinds of emotional issues. These circumstances replaced summer travel, internships, jobs, or just relaxing. As a student, suppose that you do not have the mental capacity or support system to overcome negativity, failure, disappointment, betrayal, or criticism. What can you do? My advice is for you to say, "I will not let people or events conquer me. I shall overcome."

Over the years, I have witnessed several students persevere despite challenges and circumstances beyond their control. In one instance, there was a young lady who broke her leg two weeks before exams during the first semester of her senior year. This medical emergency would allow the student to medically withdraw for the semester, receive a grade of "I" in her classes and complete the work and exams at a later time. She did not choose to do so. Instead, she remained enrolled. She made up the few days of classwork she missed immediately after she broke her leg. Her peers assisted her in getting to and from classes each day and she completed all of her exams. Despite the pain and inconvenience of it all, this young lady persevered and completed the semester with all passing grades.

Another situation of perseverance I witnessed involved a young man who lost his mother to cancer during his freshman year. The student was grief-stricken, but he chose to continue his journey toward a college education. Many of his family members encouraged him to take a break from school so that he could grieve appropriately. His response was that he wanted to make his mother proud by staying on track and he did just that. The semester in which his mother passed, his grades dropped a little, but the next semester, they were back up. With the support of his family and friends, he graduated with honors within four years, just as he and his mother had planned.

Let's use an academic example. Suppose you are failing in math. The first thing to do is to endeavor to spend more time with math by getting a tutor to assist in your lack of understanding. The tutor may be a fellow student who is proficient in math or a faculty member. Depending on the cost, an online tutoring agency might also be helpful.

Young people, please understand that life is not easy and what you receive is not an entitlement. You have to work at it. You will have obstacles littering your path, but you cannot give up. Do not allow anyone to dissuade you from the path that you set. Learn to persevere despite the odds because perseverance is one of the keys to success.

I had an uncle that I called "Big Daddy." His name was Ed Hollinger and he owned a barbershop in my hometown. Whenever anyone entered the shop, he would ask how they were doing. If they talked about some minor achievement, he would say, "That's good, but I think that you can do better. Ninety-nine and a half won't do; you gotta make a hundred." He would say this to me often. It was his way of encouraging those he encountered to persevere and do their very best. You should never stop striving to do and be the best! That is what perseverance is all about.

CIVILITY

Civility in the United States is at the lowest level that anyone has seen in decades. Our society is polarized today more than ever before. Many think, and I agree, that this polarization and incivility is being promulgated and led in the main by those involved in politics and the media. If anyone doubts or questions that our political system is broken, I ask them, as a start, to observe what's going on in Washington, DC, for just one evening. What you will see is whichever political party (Democrats or Republicans) that is in the majority in the House of Representatives, the U.S. Senate, and the White House running roughshod over the minority party. There is little, if any, politeness, respect, or compromise. There is partisanship. There is little balance. Instead, there are hyperbolic behavior and outright lies coming from both sides. Politicians, their staff, and paid party advocates across the political spectrum along with their followers paint their opponents as the enemy. The result is that no matter who wins an election, both sides harbor ill will toward the other which furthers incivility in our society. This behavior should stop!

It is important for citizens to be aware of what is happening politically. I do not support the notion of dogmatically supporting only one particular political party. I am a political independent. When I was nine years old, my father told me, "There are good people and scoundrels in both parties." Therefore, he admonished me to "support the person and not the party." This is the advice that I have carried with me throughout my life, supporting only those political candidates who support the interest of my community and institutions that I respect and cherish. I recommend this thinking to any and all who may be reading this book.

When it comes to voting in political elections, there are vast numbers of Americans not registered to vote, and a large group of registered voters who often choose not to exercise their right to vote. Many express that they do not see the importance of voting because the representatives are just "lap dogs" of the leader of their party. I regret this notion.

To me, there are two main reasons to vote. They are listed below:

1. To participate in the governmental process so that you have input in the decisions being made that will affect your life in some way.
2. To acknowledge the sacrifices made by those who marched, were beaten, went to jail, and died so that all Americans would have the right to vote.

Having grown up in the Deep South, I recognize and understand there were many sacrifices made so that I could have the right to vote. Therefore, I take my right to vote extremely serious and encourage all citizens to do the same. I believe that, whenever possible, you should always be an active participant in each process that has an impact on your life. Being aware of the workings of the political system is a part of the journey of life-long learning.

INCIVILITY

The COVID-19 health pandemic can again be used as an example of incivility in politics. Health-care officials, along with federal and state governments intensified efforts in the United States to prepare for an outbreak when it became clear that the virus would hit this country. One would not know the extent of the preparation by following the rhetoric promulgated by some politicians and media personalities on certain TV channels and newspapers. They constantly vilified the politicians and the party that did not make up their ideological preference.

The language used by both political sides was shameful and it was wrong. The pointing of fingers; the spreading of falsehoods; and the blame game seems to be the order of the day. The fact is that individuals, particularly politicians and media personalities, on both sides of the political spectrum have been guilty of spreading traceable lies. These actions are clearly dividing the country.

This practice should stop, because it is wrong and leads to heightened incivility in our country. Instead of attacking those with whom they disagree, politicians, reporters, and other media personalities should be working together to inform the public as to the true situation and what steps are being planned and implemented to prepare the citizens in the event that there is another outbreak. Reporters should just report the facts and leave the opinions to the editorial page editors.

This virus is serious, and the politicians and their ideological partners in the media should coordinate all efforts toward solving the crisis and calming fears rather than playing to their negative incivility toward each other. One solution might be for the three individuals with the most political power (i.e., the majority and minority leaders in the House and Senate, along with the President) to sit down with someone like Pastor Joel Osteen and work something out. I promise you, ideologues from both sides need help.

It has not always been this way. In the past, individuals from both parties would fight vigorously to get elected so that they could work on behalf of their constituents. Currently, it seems that the politicians govern for their respective parties, instead of governing for the people.

In the U.S. Congress today, the majority leaders or bosses tell the other elected officials what they should do and when to do it. The other representatives seem to obey like "lap dogs" and do what they are told to do. Some citizens have wondered why these "lap dogs" should be elected if they are not going to be an independent voice for their district. Still others have increasingly discussed term limits as a way to get the "do nothings" out of office. Mark Twain said that politicians are like diapers. They must be changed often and for the same reason. I think that Mark Twain was onto something.

Another aspect that also must be stopped deals with money in politics. Billionaires and millionaires have spent hundreds of millions of dollars of their own money to elect candidates in multiple states where they are not even residents and obviously do not vote. These ultra-wealthy individuals are spending this kind of money in order to elect politicians who will support their ideological agenda. Some of these same wealthy individuals have spent additional hundreds of millions of dollars in an attempt to get themselves elected to public office. For example, before dropping out of the 2020 Presidential race, one candidate was reported to have spent almost one billion dollars on his campaign. Although legal, many believe that it is nothing more than an attempt to BUY an election. To me, this is a clear assault on our democracy. Politicians and political parties seem to have forgotten Abraham Lincoln's thoughts as expressed in his famous Gettysburg Address which stated, "Of the people, by the people and for the people." Some of these ultra-rich ideologues have misinterpreted, "by the people," with "BUY the people." Unfortunately, it is currently legal to spend this kind of money on television, radio, and online advertising; political action committees (PACs); robo calls; and direct support to the candidates and their campaigns.

As mentioned in the chapter entitled "Financing Higher Education Today," *Citizens United v. Federal Election Commission* was a United States Supreme Court case which concluded that corporations, labor unions, non-profits, and others could spend an unlimited amount of money to support or defeat a candidate for political office. It was a split decision with many, including then-Senator Obama, who were opposed. At the time, the future President stated that the decision, "gives the special interests and their lobbyists even more power in Washington."[21] Later, as President, he changed his mind, but I agree with Senator Obama and not President Obama and strongly believe that Congress should pass a law which restricts the unlimited access by candidates to funding from rich corporations, PACs, and individuals.

REDUCTION OF INCIVILITY

To assist with reducing incivility in politics and the media, I propose a three-step solution. The first step deals with what is clearly too much money in politics. My recommendation is that there should be a cap of no more than $20,000 spent on any one candidate and/or their campaign by any one individual, their surrogates, or their organizations. The $20,000 cap includes any and all support.

The second step deals with a need for term limits for the members of the House of Representatives, U.S. Senate, President, and the U.S. Supreme Court. The President already has a term limit, but the others mentioned do not. Therefore, one option to consider is listed below:

House of Representatives	6 years
U.S. Senate	12 years
President	8 years
Supreme Court Justices	14 years

Such a plan would allow good people to be elected or appointed for a specified time; serve their country; and then return to private life where they could openly support their communities and families with knowledge and distinction.

The third step deals with the media. With its twenty-four-hour news cycle, the problem is exacerbated. The cable news organizations should be communication vessels, not propaganda machines. One rarely sees straightforward, impartial news anymore. In the past, most newspapers and TV networks would report the news in an objective manner. The opinions and editorializing would be reserved for the editorial pages and the opinion time slots. Not anymore. The cable channels have changed this objectivity and professionalism. In practically every news article or TV report, there is political bias and even political activism.

Unfortunately, some news outlets allow reporters to inject their biases and past negative personal experiences into a present-day story. I believe that journalism is better off when media executives do not allow reporters to bring their own personal feelings, past trauma experiences, and/or biases into a current news article. These biases taint the story and should not be allowed. This is not the professional world of journalism in which I grew up. Every news organization should have an editor or executive whose job it is, even if there are other duties, to ensure that journalistic standards are met. Further, I would like for the editors and media executives to ask themselves, "Where has civility gone? How have I contributed to the increasing incivility?"

As a teenager and young adult, I was taught, first by my mother and father, that the role of the press was important and that freedom of the press was sacred. Many people do not feel that way today and the press itself is mainly responsible for the erosion of trust. At one point in the history of our country, the mainstream press was the legitimate watchdog for the public. Now, however, they are complicit in advancing a particular ideology. Current media personalities seem to be obsessed with negativity. It does not take much to discern whether a particular channel or newspaper supports a particular point of view. There is a culture of biasness and negativity and this culture is detrimental. It is wrong when the only stories or individuals that are highlighted are those who support the narrative that is promulgated by a particular national or local news outlet. There is too much incivility in our country today and when those in the media vilify those who they do not agree with, they only give permission for prejudice.

A solution to correct this obvious prejudice starts with those who are responsible for the press (i.e., the CEOs, publishers, editors, and other media executives). These supervisors should do their jobs and advise the reporters as to what the character and culture of a first-rate news organization should be. The appropriate editors should review with the reporters the professional responsibilities relating to balance, objectivity, and fairness in any story that they may submit. If they do not do this, it does a disservice to the public and the profession of journalism as well.

Another option that may be helpful with this very dangerous bias is for every journalism school in America to offer a required course in journalistic ethics standards and principles. Such a course would teach that a reporter should utilize only facts that had been checked for accuracy from multiple sources. An ethical and educated reporter would not write a controversial story with only one source whose judgment might be tainted.

I asked a former editor-in-chief and publisher of two large newspapers why management allowed such unprofessionalism. The immediate response was, "with so many newspapers reducing their staff in some instances as much as 40-50 percent, going out of business, seeking Chapter 11 status, and consolidating, it's all about ratings and the financial bottom line." That is a shame! There are those who are more interested in the finances than the integrity of the product. This kind of executive behavior is clearly contributing to the incivility that is poisoning our country.

A third option that might bring positive results would be for a major foundation or a conglomerate of foundations to appoint a Blue Ribbon Commission with a charge to examine the very poor state of affairs that exists with the media today and recommend standards that would be required in order to keep a license and enjoy the protections that the Constitution provides. The committee can be made up of publishers and editors from the following: three of the top circulated newspapers in the country; three editors from smaller newspapers not located in large cities; the CEO from CNN and FOX; the CEO from ABC, CBS, and NBC; nine civilian CEOs from business, industry, and higher education; and chaired by a non-media person.

There's nothing sacrosanct about the twenty-one recommended members or where the individuals come from, but what is needed are individuals who are concerned about the country, courageous, articulate, and intellectually honest. The men and women of the committee should be given the funding and the staff that is needed so that they might analyze the situation thoroughly and issue a report outlining their findings.

This has actually been done before with very little positive results. Henry R. Luce, who was the founder and publisher of *Time*, *Life*, and *Fortune* magazines, actually put up $200,000 in 1942 to fund such a panel. He chose the president of the University of Chicago, Robert Maynard Hutchins, as the chair of the panel which had other big-time names such as the poet, Archibald MacLeish; historian, Arthur Schlesinger; philosophers, Reinhold Niebuhr and William E. Hocking; law professor, Zechariah Chafee; and political scientist, Charles Merriam.

Luce initiated this analysis in 1942 and it was not until 1947 that a report on their deliberations, *A Free and Responsible Press*, was published. The fact that it took five years with little or no results suggests that these important and busy individuals did not delve as deeply as they could have done. The report did not make much of a splash which also suggests that these high-powered, busy individuals did not prioritize their work. Many years after its publication, one journalist, I. F. Stone, said that the report was "a lot of high-class crap."[22] If anyone takes my suggestion seriously, I hope that this time around the outcome will be different.

Social media organizations and many of their users are also the tools of incivility which means that they are not any better. They may have aggravated the situation by allowing literally millions of individuals to publicly express themselves with few filters or checks as to the accuracy of their posts. Some platforms that conduct surveys and polls allow the user to vote multiple times each day. Obviously, the validity of these polls is illegitimate and not worth mentioning the outcomes. Those that have instituted some checks seem to be only interested in checking those entities whose point of view they do not share. Because the parent organizations provide little or no oversight, I predict that they will soon become subject to some form of federal regulations, or the federal protections that they now enjoy will be removed. In my judgment, regulations may be the only solution to insure the accurate facts on promulgation on these platforms.

Some colleges and universities are also responsible for promoting incivility. Presidents, vice presidents, deans, faculty members, and others apparently do not see the value of integration and inclusion. Why do I say this? Some institutions provide separate residence halls or floors for African Americans; LGBTQ students; those who are tofu and kale lovers; and thank goodness, those students who desire a study-intensive area. In 2021, one well-known, major university even offered six additional graduation ceremonies based on race, sexual preference, first-generation, or income level of the students. These kinds of actions make me think that we are going back to what so many of us fought vigorously against (i.e., legalized segregation).

Don't these CEOs and other leaders understand that no institution or person should separate those with differences or discriminate against anyone? Blacks, Whites, men, women, young, old, gay, or straight deserve the same opportunity to grow, develop, and enhance their learning that our colleges and universities are supposed to provide.

This promotion of learning and civility that I speak of is best provided in an open, integrated, and inclusive environment for a multitude of reasons. In addition to the chief reason being the enhancement and development of the individual personally, integration and inclusiveness is the kind of world that will await them upon graduation.

The incivility that has been promoted by politicians, the media, and some in higher education, has infected the wider community, particularly the young people. A survey entitled "Civility in America: A National Survey" conducted by Weber, Shandwick, along with Powell Tate & KRC Research found in 2016 that a whopping 75 percent believed that incivility in the United States was of crisis proportions and 56 percent felt that it would get worse. That 2016 report indicated that 87 percent attributed negative consequences at home or on their jobs to incivility.[23] Three years later, in 2019, the same research firm reported that those who felt that the United States had a civility problem has risen to 93 percent and 68 percent were of the opinion that it was a "major" issue.[24] As can be seen from the reporting, these numbers will change, but clearly we have a problem. The following chart identifies the negative impact that incivility has on our society.

Some Consequences of Incivility[25]

Incivility leads to . . .	Agree a lot/a little
Online bullying/cyberbullying	89%
Harassment (verbal, physical, or sexual)	88%
Violent behavior	88%
Hate crimes	88%
Intimidation and threats	87%
Intolerance	87%
People feeling less safe in public places	87%
Discrimination and unfair treatment of certain groups of people	84%
Less community engagement	79%
Feelings of isolation and loneliness	78%

The Civility in America survey found that social media also plays a large role in the incivility that we are experiencing in the country. Some 63 percent of all Americans, while a surprisingly 56 percent of Gen Zs (ages sixteen to twenty-one) thought that social media was more negative than positive. The chart below outlined the responses by category.[26]

Effect of Social Media on Civility

	Positive	Negative	Equally Positive and Negative	Not Sure
All Americans	9%	63%	19%	9%
Men	11%	65%	15%	9%
Women	7%	62%	21%	10%
Gen Zs (16–21)	15%	56%	24%	5%
Millennials (25–38)	11%	52%	24%	13%
Gen Xers (39–54)	6%	65%	21%	14%
Boomers (55–73)	6%	71%	14%	9%

The incivility problem is so severe that I believe that there should be a concerted effort by all segments of our society to correct it. One solution is for these progressive and conservative billionaires who are giving millions of dollars to entities, organizations, and people to promulgate their left wing or right wing point of view to stop this spending and instead fund five major civility centers at designated institutions across the United States. Those centers would be required to partner with the five major networks (ABC, CBS, NBC, FOX, and CNN) and work toward journalism ethics, political maturity and honesty, and civility in all of our institutions.

Each center should start with $50 million. These funds could come from an individual or a group of individuals who could partner with each other to fund a center. I would suggest that each center be funded at a college or university with a strong financial track record so that the accountability is built in. Each center would be required to make public its financial audit and activities each year. If this was not done, the remaining funds would be returned to the donor. My hope is that a leader will emerge who will lead a movement to challenge current political norms and media bias.

My hope and recommendation is that the young people in high school and the 20 million already in a higher education institution will lead a movement to restore civility into our lives. We need to do everything we can to make our communities, nation, and world one that is decent and honorable. Since the older adults are not doing it, the younger adults could be the catalyst in starting the movement and articulating the goals. Such an effort could be similar to the Civil Rights Movement of the 1960s which had leaders like Dr. Martin Luther King, Jr. but relied on support from college-age students of all ages, races, creeds, colors, and status. With proper direction, this latter-day movement of young people could produce leaders like John Lewis, Jesse Jackson, Stokely Carmichael, Andrew Young, Joyce Ladner, Dorie Ladner, James Forman, Diane Nash, Bernard Lafayette, and others.

Today's students can start with themselves. They can become role models for others to emulate. They can smile more. They can laugh more. I promise you that smiles and laughter are contagious. By the way, it also drives the "haters" and "snakes" crazy.

CHAPTER VII

THE VALUE OF THE COLLEGE COMMUNITY

When speaking about community as it relates to college students, I define community as a group of people who have common interests. In this case, the primary common interest of the community groups I will discuss is the success of college students. Everyone connected to college students has a role to play in ensuring their success in college and beyond. There are various groups needed to create the community that provides support to college students. These community groups are both internal and external to the college campus.

This chapter offers a guide to prospective students as to the opportunities and support programs that are available to them once they enroll in the college or university of their choice. My frame of reference is Hampton University, but most institutions offer similar services. I encourage students to become aware of what is available and take advantage of the services and opportunities as needed or desired.

FACULTY

The faculty is one of the most important community groups critical to student success. It is essential for faculty members to interact and engage with students both in and out of the classroom setting. It is not enough for faculty to simply teach their classes, grade assignments, and hold the required office hours. In addition, they must have a genuine and obvious concern for students' academic and personal lives. When they see students not reaching their potential, the faculty member should address the matter with the students and encourage those who are doing well to do even better. Faculty members should challenge students and push them to do their best at all times, never settling for less. Sometimes students do not realize their own capabilities and a watchful faculty member can guide them to a level of success beyond what they might have imagined for themselves. Research has shown that when teachers raise the bar for their students, students in turn work harder to meet the mark, hoping to live up to their teachers' expectations of them. Knowing that a faculty member believes in them can change students' perceptions of themselves and their capabilities.

In my over four decades as university president, I have heard numerous stories and received hundreds of letters from students and graduates praising faculty members for believing in them when they did not believe in themselves. Recently, a student never even considered going to graduate programs in her field, but she was accepted and received a full-tuition, room and board scholarship to attend. In another situation, a faculty member selected a student who had no interest in scientific research to work on a grant-funded project. The student accepted only because he was interested in the associated stipend. At the end of project, the student discovered a love for research and went on to pursue a PhD in chemistry. Had it not been for dedicated faculty members, these students' careers would never have gone in those directions. Faculty must understand the tremendous impact that they have on the lives and futures of their students. This responsibility proves to be in many cases life changing.

The importance of faculty members to students' internal community of support does not conclude with just academic success. It is also important for students to see faculty members attend extracurricular activities, including athletic competitions, in which they are involved. Hearing professors cheer for them or seeing them in the audience at a student-sponsored event can go a long way. The mere presence of faculty members at such activities signals to students that they have support in the classroom as well as outside of the classroom. Such support helps the overall development of students and encourages them to continue to balance curricular and extracurricular activities.

Faculty should take enough interest in their students to notice and acknowledge changes, good or bad. They should be encouraging when they see positive changes and be inquisitive when they see negative ones. This helps students to understand that their community of faculty is concerned about their overall experiences at the institution. It also gives them a sense of relief to have someone to talk to about their thoughts and feelings, someone who pays attention to them and someone who cares for them.

Good faculty members reach out to their students and are always available to them. However, faculty-student relationships are a two-way street. Students must be willing to communicate with faculty members and share their concerns, issues, and problems as well as their accomplishments and successes. Students need to understand how important faculty members can be to their success in college and beyond.

Building good relationships with faculty members is key. I often say that trust is the foundation for any positive professional or personal relationship and truth is the foundation of trust. As it relates to the faculty-student relationship, both parties must trust that the other will tell the truth, no matter the situation. Students cannot lie to professors, giving false excuses about missing class and not completing assignments and expect professors to trust them and be supportive of them. On the other hand, professors cannot lie to students or mislead them about assignments or grades and not follow through on commitments to assist students and offer additional help. When both the students and the professors build a relationship where both are truthful to one another, recognizing that the end goal is student success, their interactions will be much more positive.

Faculty can assist students in maneuvering various aspects of college life. This is why it is so important for students to build strong relationships with faculty. They can be helpful in more ways than students can imagine. Faculty members are more willing to write recommendation letters for jobs and graduate schools for students who have engaged with them than they are for those who come to class, rarely participate, and leave. When faculty members know how committed students are, they will call on others to assist students seeking internships, scholarships, and jobs. Faculty members will vouch for students with whom they have built a relationship and share opportunities with them that they might not have otherwise been aware.

A second significant and essential constituent group on any campus is the men and women who make up the administrative leadership and staff team. They are key community players in student success. When the administration and staff throughout the institution make student success a priority, they create programs designed to assist students in achieving their best. In order to enrich students' experiences and maximize student-learning outcomes, institutions must provide them with the tools necessary to be successful both in and out of the classroom.

STUDENT SUPPORT PROGRAMS

Students need supportive resources and programs that encourage academic success, persistence, retention, and graduation. Such programs may include academic support services, counseling, career planning, and student leadership. They are designed to determine students' strengths, challenges, and match students with the resources and courses that they need to excel. Support services and opportunities may include student activities, athletics, student organizations, disability services, testing, and service programs such as Talent Search and Upward Bound that are invaluable in the promotion of learning. These programs assist students in becoming acclimated to life on campus and engage them in various extracurricular activities and programs.

Ten such programs are reviewed in this chapter. My references come from personal knowledge of goals and objectives of these types of programs along with conversations with supervisors and colleagues who currently staff these entities. Though all of these initiatives may not be available at a particular college of interest, some of the services and support mechanisms that Hampton University uses can serve as a guide to students, parents, and indeed other institutions. These types of programs have a critical role to play in both establishing the basis for that common awareness and in providing students the exposure necessary to make intelligent, informed choices concerning their future.

Freshman Studies Program

Many entering students view college merely as a continuation of high school; relatively few have any real concept of the potential it offers for their individual development; fewer still have a clear understanding of how best to take advantage of that potential. Some never do learn, as reflected by high freshman attrition rates, and most learn too late to derive the maximum benefit from the opportunity that college represents.

With the growing emphasis on accountability in recent years, an increasing number of institutions unwilling to accept the consequences of their failure to address this problem vigorously and effectively have instituted orientation courses designed to help freshmen take best advantage of their first year and establish a basis for their future success. Many of these programs are dedicated to providing a comprehensive core of academic support services that will influence academic achievement and retention. These types of offerings provide meaningful, coherent, and fulfilling experiences to increase the retention rate of new students by facilitating activities such as an orientation week, academic advisement, academic counseling, mental health counseling, social and personal growth, seminar series featuring certain topics, and many other activities.

As a part of these programs, entering freshmen and transfer students may be required to participate in an intensive orientation program one week before the beginning of classes. The primary goal is to assist new students in their transition from high school or from another institution of higher learning. Through a program of structured activities, students learn about the university and their new university becomes aware of and responsive to the needs of its new students. There is a deliberate accent on the values and traditions of that particular institution so that all new students will embrace its rich heritage and perpetuate its legacy.

Some universities offer a specific course designed to introduce entering freshmen to the types of subjects that will foster and facilitate their transition to the college environment and their adjustment to the choices and challenges related to the intellectual, emotional, and aesthetic components of the type of student life that they will experience. Further, the particular university's community of scholars acknowledge the awareness of the need for educated individuals in our contemporary society, irrespective of their personal aspirations or particular career goals.

At Hampton University, for example, there is a course called University 101. It is designed to provide a holistic, well-rounded knowledge of life. Topics that are covered include Hampton University: Its History, Legacy and Future; African American Art, History and Literature; Non-Western Music and Art; English Literature; Test Anxiety; The Nature and Logic of Science; The Need for Good Personal Behavior; Time Management; Student Skills; Relationships; Career Development; Research Development; Personal Finances; Large and Small Business Development; Technology; Nutrition and Diet; and the Effects of Drugs and Alcohol on Academic Success. Additionally, these new students are encouraged to attend a series of seminars addressing writing skills, time management, mathematic skills and techniques, and test-taking skills.

Faculty and staff in this program monitor all new students' midterm and final grades. Students with academic deficiencies are placed on probation or a reduced workload and must attend the spring semester seminar series. Academic counseling focuses on ways of improving academic performance and on strategies that foster positive attitudes, improved study habits, and alternative programs of study. Strategies may include the development of time management schedules, as well as testing and note-taking techniques. Academic counseling may also result in referrals for tutorial assistance.

Health Centers

The primary purpose of health centers is to provide health care for the student population. This role begins with the necessity of students getting a medical clearance even before they physically enroll. Medical clearance is important for the health of the individual as well as the campus community as it relates to preventing or decreasing the risk of having an outbreak such as measles, which is currently impacting several college campuses across the United States.

Upon their arrival on campus, most Centers provide health care and outpatient primary care to the entire student population. Most of the care deals with episodic illnesses and some chronic illnesses such as seasonal allergies, colds, flu, upset stomachs, skin conditions, minor injuries, and reproductive health and screening tests, as well as lab testing and screenings for common illnesses.

These Centers also provide referrals, when necessary, to specialists on or off campus. Some of the on-campus resources that students may or may not be aware of include a Student Counseling Center, an Office of Disability Services, and a Title IX Office. There may be an on-call nurse available twenty-four hours a day, seven days a week.

Health education is an important part of a Health Center's role as well. This includes educating the campus community about dating violence, HIV screening, alcohol and substance abuse, nutrition, bullying, building healthy relationships, weight management, reproductive, women's, and mental health. These things are accomplished by messaging the campus community; holding resident hall meetings; and sending flyers dealing with such things as frostbite, extreme heat, hypothermia, and mosquito bite prevention.

A well-functioning campus Health Center is quite an asset to any university community. In addition to traditional health services, such a center could provide a program on stress reduction. Other activities such as yoga and the "Blow Bubble Not Smoke Event" could be offered. Yoga is a great exercise which improves concentration, sleep, and helps to manage stress. The blow bubbles activity encourages students to blow bubbles with bubble gum or bubble machines or bubble wands instead of smoking.

Institutions vary in the scope of their initiatives and size of their staff. It does not matter if an institution has a program large or small. What does matter is that a health center provides good and comprehensive health care for its students.

Counseling Center

A well-run counseling center provides individual mental health therapy for students who come in with issues relating to family; dating relationships; finances; roommate, academic and social issues; and general stress. These issues are not unusual because, nationally, psychologists and psychiatrists are reporting an increase in mental health conditions.

The national average for the utilization of counseling services at a medium size institution is 8–10 percent of the student population. Most centers offer crisis appointments and walk-ins, allowing students to receive the services that are needed in a crisis situation.

A unique aspect of some centers is that services are offered twenty-four hours a day, seven days per week. Someone is always on call and available to meet the needs of the students. Additionally, if a student needs to be hospitalized for medical or psychiatric reasons, or just needs to be assessed, a member of the counseling team actually accompanies them to the hospital. They remain with the student until they are released. Another part of the protocol should be to contact the parents with the cursory information about the hospitalization, although counseling center personnel cannot go against HIPAA guidelines. Most parents have expressed gratitude, especially if they are in states that are four, five, or six hours away from campus. As a part of their gratitude, many parents have stated that this shows that the institution is a family and is a part of their village.

Group therapy may also offer and give students a feeling of community because they do not feel so alone if they have the opportunity to connect to each other. This is especially true as it relates to depression and trauma. Students helping other students have resulted in more resilience and higher graduation rates among those needing help.

Title IX Office

Title IX of the Education Amendment of 1972 is a federal law that prohibits sexual discrimination at any institution receiving federal funding. If an institution receives federal funding, it must have a Title IX Coordinator along with a process that investigates sexual discrimination; misconduct; harassment; assault and exploitation; domestic dating violence; and stalking. Hampton University has an attorney who is an experienced Title IX Coordinator, along with a policy designed to ensure a safe environment.

Hampton University's policy calls for a rapid response once a potential Title IX incident has been reported. All services provided by the Title IX Office are tailored to students and the completion of their education. The responses include, but are not limited to, the following.

► Honoring a student's request NOT to move forward with a **Formal Investigation**, and therefore the case is then closed. Sometimes there are those who criticize the lack of activity without knowing that the alleged victim has requested not to continue.

► Reaching an **Informal Resolution** facilitated by the Title IX Coordinator, with intent to participate and options provided to be agreed upon by both parties.

► Providing **Interim Measures** while an incident is being investigated. Interim Measures are based on the incident and needs of the student. The Title IX Office at Hampton partners with the Student Counseling Center, Student Health Center, Hampton University Police Department, University Chaplain, and the Office of the Provost and Chancellor to help facilitate and provide academic accommodations, a safety plan, counseling, health screenings, housing relocation, or other similar accommodations.

If the Reporting Party in an incident wishes to move forward with a formal investigation, all parties involved will be interviewed by the professionals in the Title IX Office to gather facts of the incident, any supporting evidence and possible witnesses. In the initial intake interview, the parties are provided oral and written information about Title IX and the policies and procedures at Hampton University. Both Parties are issued a "No Contact Order" and it is emphasized that retaliation is prohibited in any form. Following the interviews, the Title IX Coordinator writes an Investigative Report based on the facts and evidence gathered. The Investigative Report is then submitted to the Sexual Discrimination and Misconduct Committee (SDMC) for a hearing and adjudication of the matter. Title IX personnel are not involved in any aspect of the SDMC deliberations. The SDMC deliberates and determines if a Title IX violation has occurred, then imposes sanctions. The decision of the Committee is final and the case is closed.

Residence Life and Housing

In general, Residence Life and Housing personnel are responsible for housing programs, including monitoring Online Housing Portal for assignments and billing through a centralized data entry system. This insures the fair and equitable management of the housing process for new and continuing students. The staff focuses on assisting students as they adjust or become acclimated with acceptable standards for student conduct and university community interaction. This group of professionals strive to provide leadership in planning, establishing, and operating the residence hall housing programs for all students, while managing all aspects of the operational budgets of their respective areas, in support of the overall student life program.

Additionally, Residence Life and Housing programs provide leadership and supervision for residential, graduate and office staff, student resident assistants, and a cadre of volunteers in several capacities. The staff advises student groups, serves on committees, supervises and provides team leadership for special projects, and assists with university-wide activities, such as registration, formal academic occasions, conference utilization of residential facilities, and other tasks.

Office of Student Activities

An Office of Student Activities is responsible for planning student activities and programs for their university community and for coordinating the co-curricular activities for students. Specifically, the members of the team should provide guidance and materials to students who are interested in joining and organizing campus organizations. Such an office has the responsibility to assist student organizations in planning activities, meetings, and projects; planning and developing student leadership workshops; updating students' Calendar of Events; and scheduling student events, securing facilities, and following institutional procedures for maintaining an effective program of student activities.

It is important for students to explore activities outside of the classroom. Soft skills like the ability to lead, manage other people, and work in teams and with others are developed through memberships in various student organizations. Many higher educational institutions have a large number of student organizations for students to join. In these cases, just about every interest can be accommodated. In some instances, if there is not an organization of interest, there is an opportunity for students to implement their own.

At Hampton University, service learning and leadership organizations play a vital role in the holistic development of students. This is done by providing community service experiences and interpersonal and leadership skills training opportunities. Service learning and leadership organizations may be associated with departments at the University that provide special services and support to the University and local-area communities. Examples of these organizations include the Greer Dawson Wilson Student Leadership Development Program (Student Activities), the Peer Counselors and Summer Peer Helpers (Counseling Center), and the Resident Assistants Association (Dean of Residence Life).

Most Offices of Student Activities have jurisdiction over the intramural sports, sport clubs, and fitness and wellness. These programs are designed to fulfill the fitness and recreational needs of students, faculty, and staff. The intramurals offer an array of team activities designed to meet the competitive and recreational needs of a particular university's community. Programs can include traditional and non-traditional team sports such as aerobics, billiards, men's and women's basketball, bowling (co-ed), dodge ball (co-ed), flag football (men), futsal (indoor soccer, co-ed), mixxed fit (co-ed), power puff football (women), men's soccer club, spades (card game, co-ed), tennis, volleyball (co-ed), women's lacrosse club, open gym, and various sports and video game tournaments.

TRIO Programs

There are four separate federal TRIO programs. They are Talent Search, Upward Bound, Student Support Services, and the Ronald McNair Post-baccalaureate Achievement programs. All are funded by the U.S. Department of Education and were created to increase college access for low-income and first-generation students. These programs provide a number of services designed to increase student persistence through college as well as graduation from college and matriculation in graduate school.

Based on campus, but serving students in their surrounding target schools, the Talent Search program is a pre-college initiative which provides academic support services, tutoring, course selection, college tours, college entrance examination prep, and summer enrichment activities for secondary students in the local city and county schools. Upward Bound provides college access and intensive academic interventions to help an annual cadre of eligible low-income and potential first-generation college students in a particular school district complete a rigorous program of secondary education and subsequently enter and earn postsecondary degrees.

Both Talent Search and Upward Bound are pre-college programs that equip participants to matriculate to college, but are not recruitment instruments for any particular university. The main goal for both programs is to increase secondary graduation rates and improve postsecondary enrollment and subsequent graduation rates from the institution that will be the best fit for each program participant.

Low-income, first-generation students and undergraduates with physical and learning disabilities are eligible for the Student Support Services program. This program has a documented record of improving the retention and graduation rates of its participants. Academic enrichment, tutoring, graduate and professional school tours, and supplemental instruction in traditionally difficult subjects such as physics, chemistry, and algebra have been enormously helpful in achieving the goals of increased graduation rates and entry into college.

Career Center

One of the primary goals of individuals attending college is to earn a degree and begin a career in their chosen field. Many university communities assist in this process by connecting students with potential employers. This connection is facilitated by a Career Center, which collaborates with campus constituents to design and deliver comprehensive career services that assist students and alumni in developing, evaluating, and implementing career plans that lead to employment and life-long personal development. A career center is the liaison between the students, alumni, corporations, and government agencies.

Hampton's Career Center offers a variety of student services that include on-campus interviewing; career consultation; cover letter and resume development and review; interview skills and evaluation; company information sessions, mock interviews, internship opportunities, an online e-recruiting system, career fairs; and a graduate and professional schools fair. Service starts with a Career Fair where freshmen are required to attend. In order to go to the Career Fair and be successful, the Career staff ensures that the freshmen have the tools that they need. This includes a resume, cover letter, and proper appearance. Some may ask "Why a cover letter?" The answer is that many companies indicate that a cover letter is not just a cover letter. It is really a writing sample designed to ascertain students' command of written language.

The students are also taught the proper handshake, the proper eye contact, and the proper appearance. At Hampton, appropriate appearance is mandatory. Some companies have commented that their representatives have gone to other well-known institutions and the students have actually come to a Career Fair in "flip-flops." Most times, the representative indicates that job opportunities are not extended to these students. Therefore, Hampton emphasizes and requires all students to dress professionally when attending a Career Fair.

A major objective in the Hampton Career Center is to advise students how important INTERNSHIPS are to their future. Internships are stressed because it is extremely important for students to start early looking for summer jobs. Many companies hire permanent employees from their pool of interns. Therefore, students are told to start freshman year and each year thereafter looking for summer internships. Some students think that freshmen cannot get internships, and they have been proven wrong. Some schools of business require their students to do internships.

I personally believe in internships because they provide the students with the opportunity to learn about themselves and how they stack up with peers from other institutions. Students can ascertain which skills and strengths are competitive and which ones need strengthening. Internships also provide the students with the opportunity to learn more about a particular company as well as that particular profession.

A very practical benefit of internships is the possibility of being hired. With this in mind, I am also an advocate of seeking multiple internship experiences. Having options are good and can help with a student's cognitive personal development and confidence.

Another big part of what Hampton's Career Center does is to teach interview skills. Students need to know what a particular company is looking for. There was a time when certain business companies would only seek business majors. That is not necessarily true today. As examples, in the past, some companies such as Accenture and KPMG would look for only business majors. Today companies are looking for skills no matter the student's academic concentration. Hampton has had students with Journalism, Social Sciences, Communication, and other majors who have gotten internships with accounting and other traditional business firms because they had the communication skills, the cognitive abilities, and the social skills that companies were seeking.

College students should make themselves aware of the many campus resources available to them as community members at their chosen institution. These resources will assist students in a successful transition to college as well as prepare them for life after graduation. All of the campus offices and programs are critical parts of an institution's support for its students.

Peer Support

Peers on campus are a significant part of the internal community of support that has a tremendous impact on student success. Students have shared experiences in their classes, the dormitories, clubs and organizations, as well as extracurricular activities. These shared experiences provide a sense of knowing and understanding among students.

It is important for students to know themselves, being aware of who they are and what they want to accomplish during college and in life. In college, students are exposed to people from different backgrounds, with different experiences and perspectives, from different parts of the nation and the world. All of these students bring with them their own sense of self and self-worth. If students are not sure of themselves, others can easily influence them. In some instances, such influence is good, but in other instances, it is not.

Students build their own group of peers while in college. Therefore, my advice is to make sure you choose the members of your community carefully! If your goal is to succeed and graduate in four years, then choose to spend your time with others who have the same goal. If you plan to succeed in class, befriend individuals who attend class regularly, not those who skip class often. If you want to make the best of your college experience, talk to students on campus who are involved in various activities and hold leadership positions. Hang out with the students who are making the best of their experience in a very positive way. If you hang out with the wrong crowd, your goal of graduating in four years might turn into five, six, or more years and/or even worse graduation might not ever happen.

Athletics Program

Athletics are popular at most institutions because they provide entertainment, camaraderie, and a positive emotional outlet for something that we are connected with if it is the home team. However, Hampton University views its athletics program as more than just competition. There is a stated goal of instilling positive values, character, leadership, hard work, teamwork, discipline, integrity, respect for one's self and others, and perseverance. The athletic administration, coaches, and staff are of the opinion that if these values are inculcated into each young man and woman, they will be winners on and off the playing field. They want their athletes to be "Leaders and Champions." Their records throughout the years have proven this philosophy is a winning one.

For a number of reasons, as articulated below, I have always been a huge supporter of the concept of student athletes: (1) Even in elementary school, my mother and father encouraged me to be active in sports after I had completed my homework. (2) My belief that the chief reason for being for any college or university ought to be the promotion of learning and athletics is a good learning tool. Think about the fact that in order to be successful in athletics, one has to be highly conditioned in body and mind. (3) One must establish goals and objectives no matter the sport's venue. (4) One must understand that teamwork is an essential ingredient in success. (5) One must understand that no matter how skilled an athlete may be, there are coaches who direct practices, individual workouts, and game plans; therefore, they must acquiesce to them. (6) Self-confidence is built by putting all these ingredients together. (7) If one is successful in athletics by embracing these concepts, one will be successful in life.

My hope is that the words, examples, and advice in this chapter have given the reader a knowledge of some of the benefits of a well-organized institution of higher education. A college or university community that is comprehensive in its offerings can provide a great deal of value to those who wish to succeed in life, both professionally and personally. Remember, contrary to what some are taught, we do not live in an entitlement society. Hard work and making the right choices are necessary ingredients for success.

CHAPTER VIII

CONCLUSION

The opportunity to attend college is a major milestone in an individual's life. Thus, being prepared improves one's chances to be successful. In the introductory chapter, I mentioned that the purpose of this book was to provide guidance on achieving success in college. In this concluding chapter, I will provide some of the "Keys to Success" that are mentioned in the various chapters of this book.

In addition to the obvious, as the names of each chapter suggests, these writings also propose innovations which will be helpful to young people in college and improve our society. While the majority of the book relates specifically to success in college, there are other areas that address societal issues, of which all readers should have some level of understanding, such as politics and the media.

I have outlined these issues using real-life examples and proposing several innovative solutions for managing them appropriately. One section provides five options as to how the $1.6 trillion dollar student loan debt can be reduced without pie-in-the-sky give-away programs. One of the options deals with my twenty-year campaign for mandatory national service. The idea is that students can help others and themselves by working, teaching, and interacting with those who may have different values, backgrounds, problems, and promises; and at the same time receive some relief from their student debt.

Second, since politics play such a huge role in the incivility problem in our country today, another innovative suggestion is to place term limits on members of the U.S. House of Representatives, the U.S. Senate, the U.S. Supreme Court, and keep the two-term limit on the President of the United States. A third is a call for a national commission comprised of media executives and representatives from higher educational institutions with journalism programs to provide guidance in major media matters which are currently negatively affecting our society. Fourth, I call for the reversal of *Citizens United v. Federal Election Commission* by reducing the amount of money in politics. Students should be aware of the massive amount of money spent on politics and how this money can be redirected.

The above-mentioned solutions as well as the keys to success outlined below will help students and parents along the path to college success.

KEYS TO SUCCESS

Preparing for College

1. Introduce the concept of college early.
2. Get involved in community organizations.
3. Engage in extracurricular activities at school.
4. Identify a mentor.
5. Enroll in a pre-college curriculum.
6. Focus on academics.
7. Develop good study habits and skills.
8. Research colleges and career paths of interest.
9. Apply to college early.
10. Make a plan for financing a college education, including completing the Free Application for Federal Student Aid (FAFSA).

Parental Guidance

1. Be a role model in character and deeds of the person you want your child to become.
2. Communicate with your children—openly, honestly, and consistently.
3. Be sure to encourage your children to exercise personal responsibility academically, personally, and professionally.
4. Be generous in serving others and inspire your children to do the same.
5. Teach and practice positive character traits.
6. Instill the concept of a good work ethic.
7. Engage in service to others.

Financing Higher Education Today

1. Research and apply for a variety of financial aid programs sponsored by the U.S. Department of Education to help students and their families with a college education.
2. Begin saving for college early.
3. Seek out and apply for multiple scholarships.
4. Accurately complete necessary federal, state, and school financial aid forms.
5. Take advantage of loan forgiveness programs.

The College Experience

1. Review statistical data that supports the recognition by parents and students of the advantages of higher education.
2. Build relationships which are critical to your future success in college.
3. Actively engage in the life of the college community which increases the likelihood of your having positive experiences.
4. Prioritize and balance your schedule and exercise self-discipline—all are essential tools for success in college.
5. Discover, embrace, and portray the following values—*character, honesty, integrity, self-respect,* and *gratitude*—that will hopefully shape you into a productive citizen for our society.

6. Hone your listening skills. That is essential to a successful college experience.
7. Avoid drugs, the drug culture, excessive alcohol, and all things related to addictive and abusive behavior during the college years.
8. Incivility has had a significantly negative impact on society and it is inherent that it be restored.
9. Remember that perseverance is a major key to success in college.
10. Set a schedule.
11. Practice good study habits.
12. Keep track of your courses and graduation requirements.
13. Get involved in clubs and organizations.
14. Attend extracurricular activities, events, and programs.
15. Step out of your comfort zone.
16. Properly balance academic responsibilities with other interests.
17. Be open-minded.
18. Practice good character.
19. Learn from your mistakes.

The Value of the College Community

1. Learn the roles and responsibilities of administrators and staff.
2. Engage with faculty in and out of the classroom.
3. Identify a mentor.
4. Utilize campus programs that offer student support services.
5. Develop sincere relationships with fellow students.

The information and recommendations in this book have given readers a blueprint for success in college and in life. The Keys to Success are simple, yet important, steps for having a rewarding higher education experience and being an informed citizen. If readers take this information to heart and incorporate it in their lives, the potential for success will be endless.

My hope is that the students, parents, and others who read *A Guide to Student Success in College* have benefited from the advice, recommendations, background issues, and innovations presented. Utilizing my training and experience for over fifty years at Talladega College, Virginia State, Harvard, Fisk, and Hampton Universities, the primary objective of this manuscript was to provide a guide to student success in college and in life. It is an honest account that may not resonate with everyone, but if the guide is followed, will be extremely helpful to individuals and our society as a whole.

In the past, particularly in the African American community, of which I am a proud and thankful part of, individuals who were neighbors, coaches, ministers, teachers, group leaders, and others provided direction as it related to values, decorum, standards, personal appearances, responsible behavior, and the like. These people were living examples of the phrase, "It takes a village to raise a child." For a host of reasons, these leadership directions are not as prevalent in our communities today as they were in the past. Hopefully, a significant number of people can be convinced that even in today's world, they can make a quality difference by speaking up and speaking out on first-class values, standards, behavior, and other issues which can lead to a better and successful life for the young and old.

Again, the desire is that this book will be instrumental in assisting a significant number of people to achieve success in college and in life. Every aspect will not apply to every person, but hopefully there will be those who benefit in a big way. Please enjoy!

NOTES

CHAPTER 1

1. Sean Seymour and Julie Ray, "Graduates of Historically Black Colleges Have Well-Being Edge," accessed August 10, 2019 https://news.gallup.com/poll/186362/grads-historically-black-colleges-edge.aspx.
2. Seymour and Ray, "Graduates of Historically Black Colleges."
3. United Negro College Fund, *The Numbers Don't Lie: HBCUs are Changing the College Landscape*, accessed August 10, 2019, https://uncf.org/the-latest/the-numbers-dont-lie-hbcus-are-changing-the-college-landscape.
4. United Negro College Fund, *HBCUs Make America Strong: The Positive Economic Impact of Black Colleges and Universities*, accessed August 10, 2019, https://cdn.uncf.org/wp-content/uploads/HBCU_Consumer_Brochure_FINAL_APPROVED.pdf?_ga=2.221982936.1957788867.1625620176-1830765113.1625620176.

CHAPTER II

1. John C. Maxwell, *Good Leaders Ask Great Questions* (Nashville: Thomas Nelson, 2014), 4.
2. Maxwell, *Good Leaders.*
3. Maxwell, *Good Leaders.*
4. Rev. Martin Luther King, Jr. "What is Your Life's Blueprint?" (Speech, Barratt High School, Philadelphia, PA, 1967).
5. Sallie Mae, *How America Pays for College 2019,* accessed January 13, 2021, https://ww2.Salliemae.com/about/leading-research/how-america-pays-for-college/.
6. Federal Student Aid, *Financial Aid Eligibility Requirements,* accessed August 5, 2019, https://studentaid.gov/understand-aid/eligibilty/requirements.
7. "FASFA Tips and Common Mistakes to Avoid," National Association of Student Financial Aid Administrators, accessed August 5, 2019, https://www.nasfaa.org/fafsa_tips.
8. Hampton University, "Hampton University Student Handbook," July 2018.
9. Anthony P. Carnevale, Ban Cheah, and Andrew R. Hanson, Georgetown University Center on Education and the Workforce, *The Economic Value of College Majors,* accessed July 27, 2019, https://cew.georgetown.edu/cew-reports/valueofcollegemajors/.
10. Carnevale, Cheah, and Hanson, *The Economic Value.*
11. Carnevale, Cheah, and Hanson, *The Economic Value.*
12. Carnevale, Cheah, and Hanson, *The Economic Value.*
13. Bennett Leckrone, "When It Comes to Future Earnings, Liberal-Arts, Grads Might Get the Last Laugh," *The Chronicle of Higher Education*, accessed January 20, 2020, www.chronicle.com/When-It-Comes-to Future/247842.
14. *The Vault Blog,* "Do Liberal Arts Majors Earn More in the Long Run?" blog entry by Derek Loosvett (September 12, 2016).

CHAPTER III

1. "Conduct and Character. A Sunday Evening Talk to the School, by General Armstrong," Southern Workman and Hampton School Record 24 (i8950): 23.
2. Anthony Rostain and B. Janet Hibbs, 2019, "Is your child emotionally ready for college?" *The Wall Street Journal* (August 24): 1.
3. F. A. Manske, Jr. *Secrets of Effective Leadership: A Practical Guide to Success* (Memphis: Leadership and Development, Inc.): 7.
4. Corporate Walmart. Our History, accessed October 12, 2020, https://corporate.walmart.com/our-story/our-history.
5. Margena A. Christian, "Johnson H. Johnson Immortalized on Forever Stamp," *Ebony* (January 10, 2012), accessed April 30, 2016, http://www.ebony.com/black-history/john-h-johnson-immortalized-on-forever-stamp#axzz47LVtS30X.
6. Martin Luther King, Jr., "Remaining Awake Through a Great Revolution" (Sermon, National Cathedral, Washington, DC, 1968).
7. Martin Luther King, Jr., "The Drum Major Instinct" (Sermon, Ebenezer Baptist Church, Atlanta, GA, 1968).

CHAPTER IV

1. Martin Luther King, Jr., "Remaining Awake Through a Great Revolution" (Sermon, National Cathedral, Washington DC, 1968).
2. Capital Group American Funds, *College America 529 college savings plan*, accessed July 15, 2019, https://capitalgroup.com/individual/products/college-america-529html.
3. Internal Revenue Service, "529 Plans: Questions and Answers," accessed July 15, 2019, https://www.irs.gov/newsroom/529-plans-questions-and-answers.
4. Voya, Tomorrow's Scholar *529 Plan Investor Guide,* accessed July 15, 2019, https://voya.com/products/tomorrows-scholar.

5. Capital Group American Funds. The College America 529 education savings plan is trusted by more than a million families, accessed July 1, 2019, https://www.capitalgroup.com/individual/what-we-offer/college-america-529.html.
6. "Google Scholarships," Google, accessed August 6, 2019, https://google.onlineapplications.net/applications/default.asp.
7. "Apply-Coca-Cola Scholars Foundation," Coca-Cola Scholars Foundation, accessed August 6, 2019, https://www.coca-colascholarsfoundation.org/apply.
8. "BK McLamore Foundation—Creating Brighter Futures," BK McLamore Foundation, accessed August 6, 2019, https://bkmclamorefoundation.org.
9. "Dell Scholars," Michael & Susan Dell Foundation, accessed August 5, 2019, https://dellscholars.org/scholarship.
10. "25 Corporate Scholarships," Top 10 Online Colleges, accessed August 5, 2019, https://Top10onlinecolleges.org/scholarships for/corporate-scholarships.
11. "College Scholarship Opportunities—Fortune 500 company scholarships," College Scholarships, accessed August 5, 2019, http://collegescholarships.org/fortune500.htm.
12. U.S. Department of Education, 2018 Federal Student Aid Brochure.
13. Abigail Hess, "U. S. Student debt has increased by more than 100% over the past 10 years," CNBC, accessed January 12, 2021, https://www.cnbc.com/2020/12/22/us-student-debt-has-increased-by-more-than-100 percent-over-the-past-10 years.
14. Lumina Foundation and Institute for Higher Education Policy, *Form & Formula: How the Federal Government Distributes Aid to Students,* accessed September 5, 2019, https://www.luminafoundation.org/formandformulas.
15. Lumina Foundation, *Form & Formula.*
16. Lumina Foundation and Institute for Higher Education Policy, *Partnerships: Where Financial Aid Began: Partnering with Campuses and States,* accessed September 5, 2019, https://www.luminafoundation.org/resources/where-financial-aid-began.

17. Lumina Foundation and Institute for Higher Education Policy, *Student Loans: How Did We Get Here? Growth of Federal Student Loans*, accessed September 5, 2019, http://luminafoundation.org/Resources/student-loans-how-did-we-get-here.

18. "Student Debt Part 2: A Brief History of Debt in the United States," Online Colleges, accessed September 10, 2019, https://www.onlinecolleges.net/student-debt-in-the-u-s-part-2-a-brief-history-of-student-debt-in-the-united-states/.

19. Lumina Foundation, *Student Loans: How Did We Get Here?*

20. Federal Student Aid, *The U.S. Department of Education offers low interest loans to eligible students to help cover the cost of college or career school*, accessed January 21, 2021, https://studentaid.gov/understand-aid/types/loans/subsidized-unsubsidized.

21. Josh Mitchell, "The Long Road to the Student Debt Crisis," *The Wall Street Journal* (June 7, 2019): C2.

22. Mitchell, "The Long Road."

23. Daniel Kurt, "Student Loan Debt: 2020 Statistics and Outlook," Investopedia, accessed January 31, 2021, https://www.investopedia.com/student-loan-debt-2019-statistics-and-outlook-4772007.

24. Josh Mitchell, Student Loan Losses Seen Costing U. S. More than $400 Billion. *The Wall Street Journal* (2021), accessed January 31, 2021, https://wsj.com/articles/student-loan-losses-costing-u-s-more-than-400l-billion-11605963600.

25. Mitchell, "The Long Road to the Student Debt Crisis."

26. Sarah Goldy-Brown, "Student Loan Debt Statistics in 2018—Student Debt Relief," Student Debt Loan, accessed June 17, 2019, https://www.studentdebtrelief.us/student-loans/student-debt-statistics/.

27. Federal Student Aid, *Financial Aid at a Glance*, accessed July 20, 2019, https://studentaid.gov/manage-loans/forgiveness-cancellation/public-service.

28. Federal Student Aid, *Financial Aid at a Glance.*

29. Federal Student Aid, *If your federal student loan payments are high compared to your income, you may want to repay your loans under an income-driven repayment plan,* accessed July 20, 2019, https://studentaid.gov/manage-loans/repayment/plans/income-driven.

30. National Association of Student Financial Aid Administrators, *NASFAA Issue Brief: Origination Fees,* accessed July 20, 2019, https://www.nasfaa.org/uploads/documents/Issue_Brief_Origination_Fees.pdf.

31. Zack Friedman, "Student Loan Repayment Is the Hottest Employee Benefit of 2018," *Forbes,* accessed July 21, 2019, https://www.forbes.com/sites/ZackFriedman/2018/10/18/student-loan-Repayment-employee-benefits/#2c9f5227566f.

32. Friedman, "Student Loan Repayment."

33. Friedman, "Student Loan Repayment."

CHAPTER V

1. "Fast Facts: Back to School Statistics," Center for Educational Statistics, accessed September 8, 2019, https://nces.ed.gov/fastfacts/display.asp?id=372.

2. "Fast Facts: Back to School Statistics."

3. "Fast Facts: Back to School Statistics."

4. "About SACSCOC," Southern Association of Colleges and Schools Commission on Colleges, accessed October 6, 2019, https://sacscoc.org/about-sacscoc/.

5. National Collegiate Athletic Association, *NCAA 2019-2020 Division I Manual,* accessed August 10, 2019, www.ncaapublications.com/productdownloads/D121.pdf.

6. "Respect: One Antidote for Shame," accessed April 12, 2014, http://lakesideconnect.com/anger-and-violence/Respect-one-antidote-for-shame.

7. Stanford Encyclopedia of Philosophy "Respect." Last modified February 4, 2014. http://plato.stanford.edu/entries/respect/stanford. Encylopedia of Philosophy.

8. John Sandford, *Bloody Genius* (New York: Penguin Publishing Group, 2019).

9. Arturo Garcia, "Here's why LeBron James might be the most generous NBA star today," *Born2Invest*, accessed September 13, 2019, https://born2invest.com/articles/lebron-james-generous-nba-star-today.

10. Dan Evon, "Has Warrick Dunn Built More Than 145 Homes for Single Parents?" Snopes, accessed September 13, 2019, https://www.snopes.com/fact-check/warrick-dunn-build-homes/.

11. Harvard Health Publishing, "Giving thanks can make you happier," accessed October 11, 2019, https://www.health.harvard.edu/healthbeat/giving-thanks-can-make-you-happier.

12. Harvard, "Giving thanks."

CHAPTER VI

1. Katelyn Newman, "Breaking Back to Meth?" *U.S. News*, accessed November 18, 2019, https://www.usnews.com/news/healthiest-communities/articles/2019-03-12/meth-from-mexico-a-growing-problem-for-law-enforcement.

2. Centers for Disease Control and Prevention, Tobacco Product Use and Associated Factors Among Middle and High School Students—United States, 2019," accessed January 30, 2020, https://www.cdc.gov/mmwr/volumes/68/ss/ss6812a1.htm?s_cid=ss6812a1_w#F1_down.

3. Linda Richter, "What Is Vaping?," Center on Addiction, accessed November 15, 2019, https://centeronaddiction.org/e-cigarettes/recreational-vaping/what-vaping.

4. Mary Beth Griggs, "Everything You Wanted to Know about the Vaping Health Crisis," *The Verge*, accessed November 15, 2019, https://www.theverge.com//2019/10/8/20899114/vaping-lung-injury-seizures-explosions-e-cigarette-youth-vaping-flavor-ban.

5. U.S. Food & Drug Administration, "Statement on Consumer warning to stop using THC vaping products amid ongoing investigation into lung illnesses," accessed October 15, 2019, https://www.fda.gov/news-events/press-announcments/statement-consumer-warning-stop-using-the-vape-products.

6. Richter, "What Is Vaping?"

7. Griggs, "Everything You Wanted to Know about the Vaping Health Crisis."

8. Griggs, "Everything You Wanted to Know about the Vaping Health Crisis."

9. Griggs, "Everything You Wanted to Know about the Vaping Health Crisis."

10. Jeremy Baver-Wolf, "Record High Marijuana Use and Vaping," *Inside Higher Ed,* accessed November 27, 2019, https://insidehighered.com/news/2019/09/09/study-college-students-using-marijuana-e-cigarettes-record-rates.

11. Griggs, "Everything You Wanted to Know about the Vaping Health Crisis."

12. Centers for Disease Control and Prevention, "Drug Overdose Deaths," accessed July 6, 2021 https://www.cdc.gov/drugoverdose/deaths/index.html1.

13. Susan Donaldson James, "How America's Colleges Are Reacting to the Opioid Crisis," NBC News, accessed December 11, 2019, https://nbcnews.com/feature/college-game-plan-/opioid-crisis-how-america-s-colleges-are-reacting-epidemic-n797696.

14. Centers for Disease Control and Prevention, "Morbidity and Mortality Weekly Report," accessed January 30, 2020, www.cdc.gov/mmwr/volumes/67/wr/mm67512el.htm?s-cid-mm6752el-w.

15. H. Hedegaard, A. M. Minino, and M. Warner, "Drug overdose deaths in the United States, 1999-2018," NCHS Data Brief no. 356 (Hyattsville, MD: National Center for Health Statistics, 2020).

16. Hedegaard, Minino, and Warner, "Drug overdose deaths."

17. Jared S. Hopkins, "21 States Reject $18 Billion Offer from Drug Wholesalers to Settle Opioid Litigation," *The Wall Street Journal*, accessed February 18, 2020, https://www.wsj.com/articles/21-states-reject-18-billion-offer-from-drug-wholesalers-to-settle-opioid-litigation-11581692527.

18. Hopkins, "21 States."

19. Janet Olsen, "Strategies for using digital technology in healthy ways," accessed February 13, 2020, https://www.canr.msu.edu/news/strategies_for_using_digital_technology_in_healthy_ways.

20. Katy Stech Ferk, "U.S. Business Bankruptcies Rose 48% in May," *The Wall Street Journal*, accessed June 27, 2020, https://www.wsj.com/articles/u-s-business-bankruptcies-rose-48-in-may-11591308842.

21. Ben Smith, "Obama on Citizens United: 'Stampede of special interest money,'" *Politico*, accessed January 4, 2020, https://www.politico.com/blogs/ben-smith/2010/01/obama-on-citizens-united-stampede-of-special-interest-money-024406.

22. Stephen Bates, *An Aristocracy of Critics* (Connecticut: Yale University Press, 2020).

23. Weber Shandwick, Powell Tate, and KRC Research, "Civility in America 2019: Solutions for Tomorrow," (December 9, 2019), https://www.webershandwick.com/news/civility-in-america-2019-solutions-for-tomorrow/.

24. Shandwick, Tate, and KRC Research, "Civility in America."

25. Shandwick, Tate, and KRC Research, "Civility in America."

26. Shandwick, Tate, and KRC Research, "Civility in America."

ACKNOWLEDGMENTS

A special thanks to Dr. Charrita Danley Quimby for assisting me with writing, editing, researching, and other support for this book. My thanks also to Dr. Joyce Jarrett for her editing and advice. Ms. Carolyn Acklin deserves a special nod for her typing and re-typing of the manuscript a number of times. I am grateful for the efforts of each of you.

To the over 37,000 students who have graduated from Hampton since I became president, please know how much I appreciate your positive representation of Hampton University.